I0766858

Hunting Tales from The Mountains of New Mexico

Hunting Tales from The Mountains of New Mexico

Robert L. Runnels

Copyright © 2020 by Robert L. Runnels.

ISBN: Hardcover   978-1-7960-7836-7
                Softcover   978-1-7960-7835-0
                eBook   978-1-7960-7834-3

All rights reserved. No part of this book may be reproduced or transmitted in any form or by any means, electronic or mechanical, including photocopying, recording, or by any information storage and retrieval system, without permission in writing from the copyright owner.

The views expressed in this work are solely those of the author and do not necessarily reflect the views of the publisher, and the publisher hereby disclaims any responsibility for them.

Any people depicted in stock imagery provided by Getty Images are models, and such images are being used for illustrative purposes only.
Certain stock imagery © Getty Images.

Print information available on the last page.

Rev. date: 12/13/2019

To order additional copies of this book, contact:
Xlibris
1-888-795-4274
www.Xlibris.com
Orders@Xlibris.com
806991

CONTENTS

LION TALES AND TRAILS

I DON'T CLAIM TO be a complete expert on mountain lions, but I have spent about 40 years observing their lifestyle. Contrary to what most people think, there are lots of lions in New Mexico. Here in Lincoln County there are way too many. Because lions are nocturnal and do most of their traveling and hunting at night, it is unusual if you see one moving around in the daylight. Thus, environmentalist-activist and game officials don't realize how many lions there are in this country.

Mountain lions are carnivores and hardly ever eat anything except fresh meat and the lion's primary diet is deer meat. Lions will take elk, antelope, bighorn sheep, turkey, and all types of livestock (lions like horse meat). Rabbits and porcupine are an occasional snack, but lions prefer deer meat to all other meat. Where deer numbers are down or in areas where deer are scarce, lions will take whatever is available.

Male lions mark their territory by making a scrape. This scrape is made by pushing back with their hind feet one at a time. He pushes up a distinct mound of dirt or debris, then urinates on his scrape. He will make these scrapes along ridge tops, rim rocks, low saddles, canyon bottoms, and along game trails. When he makes a kill he nearly always scrapes around his kill. The male lion has a large territory and normally takes 10 days to two weeks to make his circle around it. Except for detours off the beaten path to hunt when he is hungry, he will make about the same circle around his territory each trip. His scrapes serve as communication between himself, female lions, and other males and when a female in his territory encounters one of his scrapes, she will spray a bush nearby or urinate directly on his scrape. When he comes back through the area, he will check his old scrapes, freshen them and make a few new ones. By checking his old scrapes, he can tell how many female lions are around and how close to heat they are.

Lions will mate any time of the year. Lion kittens are spotted when born and nurse until a couple of months old. When the female starts weaning her kittens, (which number three or four per litter) she will carry meat to them for almost a month. By the time the kittens are three months old, the female will start moving them from kill to kill.

As the kittens grow, the female has to kill more and more often to keep them fed. After six months the kittens are about the size of a grown hound dog, and it takes a considerable amount of meat to keep them fed. The female has to kill almost every night to keep up with their growing appetites.

Lions only eat fresh meat. After a lion makes a kill, they normally will drag or carry their kill to a shady secluded spot. Then the paunch is pulled out and the lion will eat the heart, liver, and a few other choice parts. After feeding a lion will nearly always cover its kill. The lion scrapes up leaves, brush, and whatever is available from all around to conceal and preserve the rest of the carcass. During the winter the lion will return for several nights to its kill and feed. If meat spoils or becomes rancid, a lion will not eat it. This means that a single lion (male or female without kittens) will kill every time it gets hungry during the warm time of year. If a lion makes a kill tonight and it is warm tomorrow, the meat is going to spoil even in the shade. In most of the Southwest, a lion is going to kill every time it gets hungry, about eight months out of the year.

Female lions wean their kittens when they are about a year and a half old. Thank goodness, they only breed every other year. The female lion is a killing machine and extremely efficient at what she does. A grown female weighs between 90 and 150 pounds depending on whether her belly is full. It is not uncommon for a mature male with a full belly to weigh over 200 pounds.

A female lion with a litter of three or four kittens six months old will have to kill every night to keep them fed until weaning size. It's pretty simple mathematics to figure out how many deer a year it takes to keep one female with a litter of kittens fed; 250 to 300 deer a year is probably close. Where deer numbers are low, lions kill more elk and livestock. Lions are big critters and they have big appetites. A grown lion will take on 30 to 50 pounds of meat at one setting. During the winter when it is cold and meat will keep, a single lion will feed on a deer kill for several nights. Lions will eat most of the meat and consume large quantities of bone in the process. The large femur bones, larger rib bones, and back bone are usually left, depending on the size of the deer. In February 2001 Bobby York and I were hunting over on the Tucson Mountains. We found a lion kill (looked like a yearling deer) and all that was left was the paunch contents, scattered hair, and the tips of the ears. There was sign of a female and two kittens. They cleaned it up in one night, bones, hide, head, and all.

Several years back, Jimmer, (Jim Bob), a friend of mine and lion hunter from Capitan, and I found an 11-point buck that a big male lion had killed. We had a hunter with us and were hunting over behind the Three Rivers Ranch on Barber Ridge. The lion had drug the buck up under a big juniper tree, pulled out his paunch, and covered him up. The lion hadn't even fed on the deer. I have found kills like this several times before. If an ole lion feels a storm coming, he will sometimes kill and stockpile several deer. If a big snow comes, he can feed on this stockpile and doesn't have to travel and hunt in deep snow. Anyway, back to the kill Jimmer and I found... We rode by the kill early that morning. It was real cold and the scent around the kill must have been frozen. Later in the evening, we came back the same way and the dogs found the kill. We were all excited, however, since it was late evening, we decided to return the next morning. Course, we figured the lion would return during the night and give us a good starting place. We checked this kill every morning for five days. On the sixth morning there was a little fresh snow, and the ole lion had returned during the night and ate about half the buck deer. We turned the dogs loose on his track and figured the lion wouldn't go far on such a full belly. Wrong! The dogs trailed this ole lion about four or five miles back into some terrible rough country before they ever jumped him. It was foggy, wet, and miserable. Took us about four hours to get to a point where we could hear the dogs treed in one of the roughest canyons on the west side of the White Mountains. Since we were in the fog and couldn't see any landmarks, I sketched Jimmer a map on the ground to give him an idea of how the country lay below us. We decided, since we couldn't get a horse to the tree, Jimmer would take the hunter and head for the dogs on foot. I would lead the horses and circle around and meet them down canyon about a mile below where the dogs had the lion treed.

Our lion hunter on this trip was Pemble Davis from Mississippi. Jimmer got Pemble to the tree and shot the lion. It was a Big Tom. Jimmer skinned the lion and carried the hide down canyon where I met them with the horses. Pemble was pretty wet and tired, but he had a sure enough trophy lion. This had turned into a long day, after a big lion with his belly so full he shouldn't have gone half a mile. I don't think he had gone five days without eating; he must have had another kill somewhere.

Lions will eat bobcats and coyotes on occasion. They will also eat each other now and then. My Dad and I found where a lion had killed another lion, fed on him, drug him up under a tree, covered him up like it was a deer kill, and returned to feed several times. This was up near Cowels in the Pecos country of northern New Mexico. Several times we have had lions kill trapped bobcats and eat them. We hardly ever skin a lion that doesn't have porkypine quills under the skin on the front legs. Porkypine are just a snack for a lion, but they kill and eat everyone they get close to. When a lion kills a porky, he will normally just turn him over on his back to avoid the quills and eat him from the stomach down consuming everything, head, feet, and entire carcass. The porkypine blanket will be lying quills down-skin up, everything cleaned off the skin as if it had been skinned with a knife.

A mature lion has no trouble killing a grown horse or elk. I have seen lots of elk kills in the snow. and there is not much sign of a significant struggle. Along in the 1980's we pastured horses in the winter down near Tularosa on the Gardenhire Ranch. This ranch is located just west of Tularosa, next to White Sands Missile Range.

That spring in April, Jim Robinson, manager of the ranch, called and said a lion killed a horse and mule. I drove down there the next morning to have a look. The horse, a 2-year old that weighed about 700 pounds, had been dead several days when Jim found him. He got to looking around and found a mule dead, also. A lion had definitely killed both; you could see claw marks on the shoulders and teeth marks on the back of the neck. The lion tracks were also still visible in the sandy soil. Best I could decipher, the lion killed the horse first and drug him about 70 to 80 feet up into some mesquite brush. He then pulled the paunch out and ate the heart and liver. Evidently this filled him up for the time being as he had eaten nothing else. Being hot down in that area in April, the rest of the horse carcass spoiled the next day.

The following night the lion returned to feed on the horse. It was spoiled so he ventured over about a quarter mile and killed the mule. It was about the same size as the horse, maybe 600 pounds. He drug the mule up into a mesquite bush, pulled the paunch out, and ate the heart and liver. The lion evidently moved on after this, and we didn't lose anymore horses. I figure, being next to the missile range, this ole

ROBERT L. RUNNELS

lion lived on horses. At that time there were lots of wild horses on the missile range. When Jim called me, it was too late to try and trail the lion with dogs, and he didn't ever return.

Male lions will kill kittens if they have a chance. This is kind of a cat trait. Domestic Tom Cats will kill kittens on occasion. Sometimes Tom Cats will kill the male kittens and leave the females. This trait in some cats indicates a sort of protection of the hierarchy (not as much future competition from other males). It is my belief that male lions kill kittens when they can, for romantic reasons. If a female lion loses her kittens, she will cycle and come in heat sooner than the almost two years it will take otherwise.

Female lions normally raise their kittens away from males. She will fight to protect them and usually can drive a male lion away.

Tom Chaffins and I were trailing a lion one time over on the Patos Mountains. Dogs had been trailing for a couple hours and bayed up in some cliffs on a shady north hillside. The snow was deep on the shady side of the mountain that January. We left our horses and climbed up into the cliffs where the dogs were bayed up. Dogs were up under a big ledge barking into a crevice. There were some bones lying around under the ledge, and right away we decided there must be some lion kittens in the crevice where the dogs were barking. We pulled the dogs back but couldn't see anything. I crawled up close to the crack and took a picture with a flash camera. When I got the film developed, we could see three lion kittens in that crack. They looked to be three or four weeks old. Their mother had picked a good place to have them. They were safe from male lions or hound dogs. We pulled the dogs off and left; we didn't know we were trailing a female until the dogs found the den.

Tom Chaffins and I found some small spotted kittens another time on the Tucson Mountains. This time we were hunting bears in August. It had been raining for several days. We were riding along looking for bear tracks. The dogs all of a sudden started winding with their heads in the air. They ran up the hill into a thick stand of small pine trees and started treeing. We rode up there and found a small lion kitten in a juniper tree. There was a fawn deer covered up nearby that was half eaten. We looked around and found three more kittens all in trees close by. In this little stand of trees there was a large pile of pine needles about three foot high and covering an area about the size of a pick-up bed. There wasn't any meat covered up. The fawn deer was about 30 yards away. The kittens were about the size of grown house cats. All we could figure was the ole female was weaning them off milk and had carried in the fawn deer to feed them. The pile of pine needles must have been cover from the rain. The female lion had piled it up so the kittens could crawl up under it and keep dry.

I know there are a lot of self-appointed lion experts, and book-learned biologists, who will disagree with some of my philosophy. After all, my knowledge about lions was only learned in the woods observing lion tracks and sign.

I keep a few hounds and enjoy following them through the hills. Lions are not an easy critter to trail with hounds for several reasons. Lions at times don't leave much scent. Scent is a peculiar thing. Relative humidity, wind, air temperature, and ground cover all affect scent. A dog's ability to trail lions depends on lots of factors. First of all, if one is going to hunt lions, he has to look for lion sign in deer and elk country. Lions leave very little scent compared to that left by deer, elk, coyotes, and bear. We normally hunt lions during the winter when bears are in the den, so we don't have to worry much about bear scent. We do have to contend with lots of deer, elk, and coyote scent.

Hound dogs have good noses, and a good hound dog pup will trail about anything he can smell. It takes lots of training and hunting, normally three to four years, before a good lion dog starts to figure out what scent you are looking for. A good lion dog has a cold nose (can follow a faint scent), has a good voice, is stubborn on a track, and is aggressive when he needs to be. When trailing a lion, he has to trail through lots of other scent and keep his mind on the lion scent. Depending on weather conditions, a good seasoned lion dog can trail a lion track two or three days old. Other times, with poor trailing conditions, a good dog might not be able to trail a lion track two or three hours old.

A lion may travel 10 to 20 miles in one night, depending on whether he is hunting or just traveling. A lion can travel long distances at his own pace. If he has to run full out, he will tire in a short distance. Lions kill by stalking their prey. They are extremely fast for about 300 yards, and this is normally all it takes to catch a deer, once the lion slips up within striking distance.

When we are hunting lion, if we find a track dogs can smell, we try to trail him. Sometimes it's hard to tell if the lion is two nights away or

ROBERT L. RUNNELS

in the next canyon. I've trailed lions for three days without getting any closer. On the other hand, I've caught several lions within 10 minutes after finding the track.

I have been fortunate growing up in the mountains, with plenty of opportunity to hunt. My Dad, Arvel Runnels, was one of the best outdoorsmen that ever took a breath of fresh mountain air. I followed him around most of my life and learned a good deal about the great outdoors and big game hunting. I will be happy if I turn out to be half the big game hunter my Dad was.

Several years ago, my wife Sandra and I were hunting lions on the Three Rivers Ranch south of Carrizozo, New Mexico. There had been snow on the ground for four or five days. We rode over an old lion track, and the dogs could smell it a little, so we let them trail. The track was old enough the dogs could only trail on the north slopes. Sandra and I decided to ride out on top of a big ridge, so we could listen to the dogs trailing in the canyon below us. We topped out and were riding along the ridge top. All of sudden some deer crossed the ridge in front of us. The deer came from the direction where the dogs were. First thought that crossed my mind was maybe one of my young dogs had lost interest in the old lion track and was wanting to chase something fresher. Sandra was watching the deer, and I said, "Think I'll ride up there where those deer crossed and see if one of those dogs is trailing them." (Thought this might be a good chance to do a little dog training). Just as I turned to ride off, the last deer to cross the ridge stopped to look back at us. The deer, a doe, was about 150 yards away. I was riding away with my back to the deer when Sandra started hollering at me, "There's a lion; there's a lion!" While Sandra was watching the deer, a lion bounced out of the brush and caught the doe that had stopped to look at us. When I turned my horse around, the deer was bleating, and the lion had it on the ground. Sandra jerked her gun out, ran to a stump, and got a rest. Whack! She killed the lion while it had the deer down. The deer jumped up and ran off.

When we rode down to the dead lion, there was a big blood trail left by the wounded deer. I figure a coyote caught it before the night was over. This lion wasn't hungry because when we gutted it, its belly was full of deer meat. The doe just happened to stop close to where the lion was laid up, and it couldn't resist. Sandra and I were beside ourselves with excitement! This was the first lion Sandra had ever shot. And how often does one see a lion catch a deer in the wild?

As it turned out, this was the lion my dogs were trailing, except this time they got to the lion too late to see the kill. Goes to show, strange things do happen occasionally, if you hunt enough.

Another story comes to mind about a friend of mine from Shreveport, Louisiana. Steve White has hunted with my Dad and me for something over 30 years. Several years ago, Steve decided he wanted to kill a lion. Steve is quite a hunter and has hunted all over the world. We knew Steve had been through some heart surgery, so I spent several weeks trying to find some lion sign in easy country. There are lots of lions here in Lincoln County, but it isn't always easy to find one in accessible country, especially when you want to. Steve came the first time, and we rode through lots of easy country but found no recent lion sign.

Sandra shot this lion while it had a deer down.

We rode for three or four days and didn't get Steve very excited. However, he is an avid outdoorsman and enjoys seeing wildlife which is plentiful in the wintertime. When Steve left, he promised to come back the following winter. Well, in the meantime, he had more heart trouble which resulted in another open-heart surgery. He recovered fine and did return the following winter. The second hunt turned out to be almost a repeat of the first hunt. We rode three or four days and didn't

ROBERT L. RUNNELS

get a lion. Steve was getting pretty disappointed, but he had confidence in us and returned for a third hunt.

A friend and hunting partner of mine, Bill Wright from northern New Mexico, was here hunting with me when Steve returned the third time. Bill, Steve, and I rode and looked for lion sign for a couple of days with no luck. The second night, while sitting by the fireplace talking about where we ought to go the next day, Steve informed me that the riding was not bothering him. He said, "Robert if you think you know where we can get a lion, heck, let's go for it. I don't care if we have to ride farther and get in some rougher country. I believe I can make it fine."

There had been several big snows in the Bonito country, but no fresh snow for over a week. The snow that was left was mostly on the shady sides of the canyon, and it was packed and crusty. I told Steve we could ride across the mountain from Bonito Stables and get down on the West Side where most of the deer and elk were wintering. I knew there was lion sign over on Barber Ridge because Bill Wright and I had caught a lion in that area the week before.

Next morning, we left early and rode across the mountain to Barber Ridge. Snow was crusty and hard to ride on, but we busted through, dragging our stirrups in the packed snow in several shady places. Our dogs could walk on top of the crusty snow. But our horses had to lunge through up to their bellies. When we got over to Barber Ridge, I decided to let Steve rest awhile. I told Steve we would build him a fire, then Bill and I would ride on down the ridge and see if we could find a lion track. Plan was, if we found a good track we would come back and get Steve.

We had six dogs with us, and they laid down to rest while Bill and I drug up some dry wood for a fire. It didn't take us long to get a fire going, and Bill and I mounted up and started to ride off. Ole John, my best dog, had been right by the horses when we started gathering wood, but I looked around and didn't see him anywhere. I hollered and whistled and looked around, no John. It's about this time I remembered seeing some old bob cat tracks back up the trail a ways. I started thinking, "Durn, this will be my luck. Ride poor ole Steve all the way across the mountain and just when we get where we ought to find a lion track, I lose my best dog." Well, I'm about to work myself into a froth because I knew if we found an old lion track, I'd need ole John to work the track on the sunny sides where the snow was gone. Bout then Bill hollered at me and told me he can hear ole John bawling off in a big canyon to the north. Before the other dogs could hear John, I caught them and tied each to a tree. I kept thinking about that old bob cat track, and I didn't know what John might be trailing. After tying up the dogs, I rode over where Bill was listening. John was down in a big rough canyon on the shady side. I knew he had to have found the track, whatever he was trailing, somewhere close to where we had stopped.

I started walking around the hillside on the frozen snow, but I couldn't find any tracks. John and whatever he was trailing, were both on top of the frozen snow and not leaving any tracks. I decided to go get another dog and see what would happen. I turned the dog loose, and he started down the canyon toward John. Soon he was barking and trailing, too. Well, we turned a third dog loose and decided we better keep three with us. The dogs trailed around the mountain into Tanner Canyon and got out of hearing. Bill and I rode by Steve and told him to sit tight until we figured out what the dogs were after. We rode up the ridge we had come down earlier.

Steve White, Shreveport, LA, on the right holding his lion.
Robert on the left holding two good dogs, John and Joe.

Soon we could hear the dogs way down on the side of Tanner Canyon. They sounded to be treed. I told Bill to hold the three dogs and stay with the horses, and I would walk down and see what was going on. The dogs were on a steep north hillside. I could walk on top of the snow part of the time, but when I fell through the crusted snow was up over my knees. I finally got down to the dogs; they were treeing up a big Douglas fir tree. The limbs came almost to the ground. I could see the dogs under the

                    ROBERT L. RUNNELS

tree, but I couldn't see anything in the tree. I walked up under the tree, and all of a sudden, crash, dead limbs started breaking and a big ole lion jumped out of the tree on the upper side and took off around the hill. Durn, surprised the heck out of me, and, worse, the dogs didn't see him jump. I grabbed ole John and drug him away from the tree to a spot where the lion hit the ground. When I turned him loose, he ran back to the tree and started treeing again. I finally got all three dogs, John, Joe, and Jigger tied together and drug all three away from the tree and down the lion tracks a ways. The dogs finally started smelling the track, so I let them loose. This time they took off on the track again. I got my radio out and called Bill and told him we had a lion treed, but the lion had jumped out. I told him to turn the other three dogs loose, which he promptly did. It didn't take the other dogs long to come to me, and I put them on the lion track. All the dogs were soon over another ridge and out of hearing. I called Bill and told him to sit tight, and I would cross the ridge to see if I could hear the dogs. Soon as I climbed over the ridge, I could hear them treed again. I didn't waste any time getting down to the dogs. Six dogs were treeing this time, and I figured we had the lion for sure. Soon as I got close enough to see the lion in the tree, he saw me and jumped out again. The dogs saw him jump this time, and down the canyon they went, out of hearing again. I didn't have to travel far this time, and I could hear them treed again way down in the bottom of Tanner Canyon.

Tanner Canyon is almost no man's land because it is so steep and rough. Bluff after bluff, rockslides, thick brush, and steeper than a wall. With the frozen ground and crusty snow, the terrain was slicker than a glacier. Well, I called Bill and told him to go get poor ole Steve and bring him down to my horse. Then they would have to walk down my foot tracks. I decided I would wait for Bill and Steve before trying to go to the tree again. It took a couple of hours for Bill and Steve to get to me. Steve had told me earlier that he could walk downhill all right but climbing would be tough. Well, turned out even downhill was pretty tough; Steve slipped, fell, tumbled, and rolled umpteen times. Anyway, he made it to where I was waiting. We slid on to the canyon bottom and decided to slip up close enough for Steve to shoot. We got within about 75 yards of the tree and could see the lion sitting on a limb. I got Steve a rest and told him to shoot the lion through the shoulders. I knew if Steve didn't make a good shot, the lion would have plenty of time to kill several dogs before we got there. However, Steve made a good shot, and we didn't get any dogs hurt. Well, we did have the lion killed, but we weren't out of the woods yet, so to speak.

Bill and I walked back to the horses and, by leading them down and around cliffs and bad places, finally got them to the canyon bottom. We tied the lion on a horse. Bill and I both walked and led our horses. Steve wasn't able to do much more walking, so he had to ride. We worked our way down Tanner Canyon to the forest boundary and around the boundary fence to the mouth of Spring Canyon. It was dark when we got to Walker Well in Spring Canyon. I told Steve we could drag up some wood and build him a good fire, Bill and I could ride in to the stables and then drive around the mountain and pick him up. Steve considered this proposal for a few minutes, then asked, "How long will it take to get to the stables?" I told him, "'Bout three to four hours in the dark." He then asked, "How long will it take to drive from the stables around here to get me?" I told him we would have to put the dogs and horses up and feed. Then with the drive it would be about four hours. Steve figured on this a little while and said, "I'd be here waiting about eight hours. Heck, I'd just as soon ride on in. If I have another ole heart

Big lion, measures #15 Boone and Crockett. In the picture at Bonita Stables, Pat Joiner left, Arvel Runnels right. Pappy and I caught this ole lion in Lincoln Canyon, White Mountain Wilderness.

ROBERT L. RUNNELS

attack I'm going to die, snap, just like that, and actually I'd whole lot rather die here on this mountain than in some old hospital."

Well, needless to say, we all rode in and Steve made it fine. This time he had his trophy to take back to Louisiana. Steve White is one of the finest men and best sportsman I have ever had the pleasure of hunting with.

Most of our lion hunts take place during the winter. Normally the weather is cold, and the hillsides are frozen and icy. We hardly ever get to trail a lion in easy country. Lion trails nearly always lead into bluffy, steep, rough country, and we always feel lucky when we get one. We spend way more time riding and looking for sign than we do actual trailing. If we are lucky enough to find a lion track that dogs can trail, normally it's just the beginning of a long tough ride. An average lion chase, if the track was made the night before, is six to eight hours. When we do trail up and catch a lion in less than six hours, we feel like it was an exceptionally good day.

SOMETIMES IT'S QUICK

SEVERAL YEARS AGO, a hunting friend of mine, Jim Sheppard, from Edmond, Oklahoma was at my house to go lion hunting. It snowed for three days after he arrived. We sat around the house until we were about to get cabin fever. Evening of the third day, we decided to get out and look around. It was still snowing and windy. I knew it wasn't a good day to go hunting, but we needed to get out of the house. We loaded four dogs and our horses and headed out north of the Capitan Mountains toward the Ross Flatly Ranch. We unloaded just east of the ranch house and headed north toward Bear Tank. We hadn't gone half a mile, when I noticed where a lion had crossed the road, probably the night before. The track, where I could see it had about four inches of new snow on it. With all the wind and snow, it was hard to tell it was even a lion track. However, the dogs could smell it a little and wanted to trail, so we let them go. After a few minutes we couldn't hear the dogs at all because it was so windy. I started out trailing the dogs in the snow, which didn't last very long as they soon got into some rough bluffy country. We rode around the mountain to see if we could pick up their tracks on the other side. We made a big circle and didn't find any sign of the dogs. It was getting late and cold, so I told Jim we better head for the truck. I stopped by Ross Flatley's house and told him I had lost my dogs on a lion track. Ross said he would call me if they came in during the night.

About 10:00 p.m. that night Ross called and said three of my dogs were at his house. Jim and I drove out to get them. When we arrived, Ross met us at the gate and said he had put the dogs in his barn. We loaded John, Joe, and Jigger in the truck; my best dog at that time, Rattler, wasn't there. We hauled them back to town, fed and put them up for the night.

It had stopped snowing by the time we got back to the house, and the wind had let up some. I decided Jim and I ought to go back the next morning early and look for Rattler and see if we could figure out what happened. We drove up to Flatley's early the next day, and

Rattler was there. We fed him and unloaded our horses and dogs. We headed north to Bear Tank and turned up a little ridge towards Reed Mesa. All of a sudden, we rode right over a fresh lion track. The track was so fresh, it looked like he had just run from us. The dogs left out with their heads in the air on a dead run and were treed in less than 10 minutes. Jim killed the lion, and we were back to the truck in less than an hour.

I think the dogs had treed this lion the evening before. Three dogs had left the tree and came in early. Rattler had probably stayed at the tree all night. On the way out with our lion, we found a fresh deer kill. We had just happened to ride up the same ridge the kill was on. The lion heard us coming and ran from us. This was one of the quickest lions I have ever caught.

A few years later in the same area, a little northwest of Bear Tank, I caught another lion that was even quicker. Bryan Hughen from Midland, Texas was with me. It was a cold windy day and no snow, the kind of weather I normally wouldn't have hunted. Bryan was at my house to go hunting, so we headed out even though it was windy and dry. On this trip I had Rattler and John with Joe and Little Blue, two yearling pups. We were riding along about a quarter mile northwest of Bear Tank. All of a sudden, Rattler and John started whippin' their tails, bawled and headed west up the canyon. The two pups bawled and headed east, down the canyon. I knew the track had to be fresh even though I couldn't see it. I figured the two pups were backward on the track because my two old dogs had gone the opposite way. I started hollering at Joe and Little Blue, trying to call them back. I told Bryan the two pups were backwards on the track, and we would have to try and catch them and turn them around. I loped out to the edge of a little canyon, and the first thing I heard was Joe. Dang, if he didn't sound like he was treed. I figured maybe he had found a porkypine. He wasn't maybe 100 yards below us, so decided I could run get him and put him on the track the right direction. We turned our horses down the hill and hurried down to get those two ole dumb pups. Well, I could have ate my hat, when we get there; Joe and Little Blue were barking up a pine tree with a big lion in it. Bryan shot the lion; we hung him up and spent the rest of the day trying to catch up with John and Rattler who were trailing the wrong direction. This was Joe and Little Blue's

     ROBERT L. RUNNELS

first lion. Again, as luck will have it sometimes, I was hunting on a day when hunting conditions weren't in my favor. Bryan and I just happened to cross this ole lion's track about 100 yards from where he had bedded up for the day. Luckily the two pups didn't go with my old dogs. Often the weather doesn't make any difference; it's just being in the right place at the right time.

Several times I've ridden up to a fresh lion kill and caught a lion in 15 minutes. We look for lion kills all the time. Normally, it is hard to find a kill that a lion is still feeding on, especially on a cold morning. Lions cover their kills to help preserve the meat and to hide it from other predators. I've ridden within 50 yards of fresh kills several times early in the morning and not found them. That evening on the return trip, I wondered how I could have been that close and missed seeing the fresh kill. The answer is easy; early morning on a cold day a kill will be frozen and there isn't much scent. Later in the day, at a warmer temperature, dogs will sometimes smell a kill a couple hundred yards away.

If a lion has been feeding on a kill for a couple of nights, there will be lots of lion tracks around. Normally a lion doesn't lie around close to his kill. He travels around in and out, coming and going from all directions. The resulting network of tracks around a kill is extremely confusing to hound dogs.

A couple of years ago, Kevin Larabee from Meade, Kansas and I found where a lion had killed a doe and was in the process of covering it up when we rode up. We caught the lion in about 10 minutes. This past winter, 2002, Matt Brentlinger from Edmond, Oklahoma and I found where a lion had killed a cow elk and was in the process of covering it when we rode up. We caught the lion in about 15 minutes. The lion had caught the elk, a grown cow, on fresh snow. There was no sign of a struggle.

Kevin Larrabee from Meade, Kansas, and his first lion in 1999. We trailed this lion away from a fresh deer kill. Only took about 10 minutes after we turned the dogs loose.

Jim Sheppard and one of the quickest lions I ever caught. The hound dog bitin' the lion is Joe.

Robbie, Robert, Little Blue, and Bryan Hughen's lion.

ROBERT L. RUNNELS

TRAINING BEAR DOGS

LOTS OF FOLKS think that every time we ride out with hound dogs, we get a bear or lion. There are also a lot of misinformed people who think bears and lions are at a big disadvantage when hunted with dogs. Most hounds worth their keep will try to trail about anything that leaves scent. Critters that leave scent in most bear and lion country are deer, elk, coyotes, foxes, coons, badgers, skunks, turkeys, and wild hogs to name a few. It takes several years of work with a hound before he decides what scent you're after. As mentioned previously there are lots of variables that affect scent, like wind, temperature, moisture, relative humidity, and ground cover. When hounds get scent of game, they normally start trailing. They can't, however, determine which way the game is traveling. This means that 50% of the time, they may trail backwards. When hounds do get started the right direction on a bear track about half the time they will get side-tracked along the way, or out run, or the bear will just stop and whup the tar out of the hound dogs. When we do get an ole bear in a tree, we normally feel pretty fortunate. A good example, last fall and winter we kept score. In the fall the score was Bears-7 and Cowboys-2; for the winter, Lions-14 and Cowboys-2.

We spend lots of time messing with hound pups trying to break them from wanting to trail things other than bears or lions. Traits we like in a good hound dog are loud voice, cold nose, tough feet, aggressive nature, and stubbornness on a track or at a tree. Stubborn and hard-headed, this trait fits most good hounds. We breed this into them and sometimes scratch our heads when we are trying to teach them something.

This brings to mind a story about dog training that I should tell. Several years ago, I had a bunch of young hounds that were needing some training. I had let them play with a few coons and wild cats and decided it was time to teach them what bear scent was. I had a fresh bear hide in the deep freeze, so I got it out and let it thaw. I saddled my horse and carried the bear hide up the canyon, then tied my rope to the hide and drug it around the hill side a ways. Got off my horse rubbed the hide around on a big tree, then pulled it up over a limb. I then rode back to the house, necked several young dogs together and let one old dog (Homer) loose. Took them up the canyon and put Homer on the drag track. Ole Homer was a seasoned bear dog and exceptional on a tree. Well, ole Homer bellowed and took off on the track. I turned the young dogs loose and they set in after Homer barking and howling. I thought, "Boy this is going to work good." Well they trailed to the tree alright, and Homer even barked a couple of times at that ole hide. However, the ole bear skin wasn't moving or growling, and Homer lost interest pretty pronto. The young dogs did trail a little bit, but they didn't even see the hide in the tree. I gathered them all up and headed back to the house.

After thinking on this for a while, I decided I could improve on this training procedure. I should get up in the tree, wrap the hide around myself, and jump up and down on a limb and growl. This ought to excite those pups and maybe make them look up in the tree and bark a little.

I told Pappy and Sandra what I had in mind. We decided that they would give me about an hour to lay a new trail, then they would bring the dogs and turn them loose on the track. Meantime, I found some black coveralls, put them on, got my horse and headed out. I rode back up the canyon, got my bear hide, took it across the canyon, and started dragging it again. I took it around the mountain and up the canyon about a mile. Located a good tree that I could climb, left the bear hide, and took my horse off a ways. I then returned, wrapped the bear hide around myself real good and climbed the tree. It wasn't very long until I heard the dogs coming. They trailed up to the tree, and I started jumping up and down on a big limb, growling and snorting. Sure enough, those ole pups really got excited, I forgot about ole Homer, being pretty aggressive. Anyway, he got too excited and climbed right on up the tree. He was barking vigorously and snapping at my feet and legs pretty serious like. Had to kick him out of the tree several times. I sure was glad when Pappy and Sandra got there and finally tied him up. This little training method almost worked too good. Took about a week, but my feet finally healed up enough so I could get my boots back on.

TED LEMASTER'S FIRST BEAR

TED LEMASTER AND I met in 1976. Ted and his family were visiting Red River and someone told him about me so he stopped by to get acquainted. Ted and his brothers, Gary and Bruce, had coon hounds and were naturally interested in meeting other dog hunters. Ted told me he was interested in killing a bear, so we made a deal to trade for some dogs. Ted made, I think, four trips from Amarillo before we finally got him a bear. We caught a yearling one day and drug him out of several trees with a rope, just to play with the dogs a little but didn't kill him.

The day Ted finally killed a bear, we saw four bear in one canyon. This was the only bear chase I can remember when we could see the bears and dogs both and watch most of the chase. We were sitting on a side hill watching the excitement from across the canyon. We could see four bears at one time. They were milling around and crisscrossing back and forth across each other's tracks. The dogs were all confused and scattered out all over the hillside. Finally, we saw two bears climb up a rockslide and go into a big patch of fir timber close to the top of the mountain across from us. Soon, two dogs trailed out the way the bear had gone. These dogs were Bum, a Plott hound, and Go-Go Red, a Redbone-Walker cross bitch. We watched as the two hounds climbed out the way the bear had gone. They entered the big patch of timber across from us. Bum stayed in the timber, and Go-Go Red trailed on out. After listening awhile, we decided that Bum was treed. Ted and I thought we better get around there quick because one dog might not hold the bear very long by himself. As we approached the tree, the bear jumped out. We could see the bear was just standing there looking at Bum. I was carrying Ted's gun, a 30-30, because his saddle didn't have a scabbard. I told Ted to get off and shoot the bear before he decided to run off. We were on a pretty steep hillside, and I took the gun out to hand it to Ted. The old gun had a sling on it, and, as I handed it to Ted, the sling hung on my saddle horn. Ted, trying to jerk the gun loose, pulled the horse down on top of him. There was quite a scramble, but we finally got everything untangled. Meanwhile, the bear was standing patiently across the canyon about 75 yards away. Ted finally got a bead on the bear and shot. The bear just stood there looking around. Ted's horse spooked from the gunshot and sold out down the mountain knocking down the brush. Ted shucked another shell into his gun and set off another charge. By now the horse has crossed the canyon and ran right up to the bear and dog. This scared the bear, and he took off straight up a rockslide running ninety to nothing. I scratched my head and waved goodbye to the bear. I knew one dog would never tree him again. Anyway, Ted levered another round and took a quick shot at the bear running about 300 yards away. Must have been our lucky day because he hit the bear, and he came rolling back down the rockslide. The horse continued on around the mountain and out of sight. I told Ted to take my horse and stay with the bear, and I would go trail his horse up and bring him back. I found the horse about a mile away grazing on a little ridgetop. I rode him back, and we loaded Ted's bear on my horse and packed him out. The rest of the dogs were still trailing bear, but this was the only one we got. Ted, Gary, and Bruce Lemaster have become very close friends, and we have been on many good hunts since. Ted even shoots better now-a-days.

Ted Lemaster's first bear; Flag Mountain, 1977.

ROBERT L. RUNNELS

THE BEST TREE BARK I EVER HEARD

D URING THE WINTER of 1977, while I was living at the Questa Ranger Station, I decided to take a little vacation and go to Texas lion hunting. It was mid-December and getting close to X-mass time. So, I took a couple of weeks' leave, loaded seven dogs, and headed for Amarillo. My ole hunting pardners, Bruce, Ted, and Gary Lemaster met me in Amarillo, and we headed for Southwest Texas to do a little lion hunting.

We made camp and circled around looking for lion sign for a couple of days. We found plenty of old lion sign, but nothing fresh enough to track. An old friend of mine from up around Wichita Falls came down to hunt with us a few days. His name was Cliff Hitchcock, and he had been wanting to kill a lion for years. Well, the first couple of days he wasn't too impressed as we hadn't even been able to get a single bark out of those ole hound dogs. The Lemaster boys had gone back to Amarillo. The third night, Cliff had to go to town for some reason or other. On his return to camp a couple of hours after dark, a lion ran across the road right in front of him. Cliff came roaring into camp so excited he could barely talk. Best I could gather, where he saw the lion wasn't very far from camp. We loaded six dogs in the pickup, and Cliff took me back to show me where the lion crossed the road. It was a real dark night, no moon whatsoever. The lion had crossed in a narrow spot in the canyon and gone up an ole steep bluffy hill side. It would have been hard to climb in the daylight. I took Red out of the pickup and let him loose to check the situation out. He hardly hit the ground when he bawled and headed across the creek. I turned the rest of the dogs loose, across the creek, and up through the bluffs they went. They didn't go maybe half a mile, but almost straight up. We listened for a while and decided they had split up. Red and Bum sounded to be treed, and my young dogs were trailing back down towards the canyon bottom. I figured those young dogs had probably found a fresh coon track. They hit the canyon bottom baying and making all kinds of racket. All the dogs down the canyon were young so I didn't pay them much attention. Red and Bum were treeing up there on the hillside. I looked through my pickup, and all I could find was one old flashlight, with the batteries near dead. The dogs weren't far up the hillside, so Cliff and I headed to them. It was pretty slow climbing up those bluffs and through all the brush with one dim flashlight. However, we made it up to the dogs. They were treeing up a big tree, just below a sheer cliff on a little bench. Dogs were real excited, but with my dim flash light I couldn't see the lion. I took the flashlight and climbed up in the tree, still couldn't see the lion anywhere. The other dogs were still barking way down the canyon below us. Red and Bum were acting more and more like they wanted to go see what all the excitement down the canyon was about. I took a little rope and tied ole Red to the tree. I told Cliff he would have to stay there with the dogs, and I would go back to camp and get a better light. When I started to leave, Cliff stopped me and asked, "What if the lion decides to jump out of the tree?" I told him he did not have to worry; as long as the dogs kept barking the lion would stay in the tree. About this time, I noticed Bum had left and gone down the canyon to the other dogs. However, ole Red was still treeing like a champion. Cliff still seemed a little bit hesitant. Before he could change his mind about staying, I took our little dim light and headed down the mountain. When I got down to the road, I stopped to listen. I couldn't hear ole Red treeing anymore. All at once I heard something jump in the back of the pickup. Yep, you guessed it, ole Red had chewed his rope in two and followed me to the truck.

It was awful dark and quiet up on the hill. All of a sudden, I heard Hitchcock cut loose, "woof, woof, woof, woof," treeing like nothing you ever heard. Now, he was really cutting loose. Sounded better than any hound dog I ever heard. I got in my pickup, turned on the spotlight, and shined it up on the mountain; there was the lion still sitting in the tree. When I got back to Hitchcock, he was still treed solid. I told him he could quit barking because the lion was about 50 yards on up the hill in another tree. As the saying goes, "He was barking up the wrong tree."

This lion was very cooperative as he stayed in a tree on a bluff for about two hours without a single dog under the tree. I studied this scene the next day in the sun light. The reason there weren't any dogs under the right tree was because of a bluff that the dogs couldn't climb to get to the tree.

After Cliff killed the lion, we hauled it to camp and hung it in a tree. On the way back down the canyon, I stopped and called my other

    ROBERT L. RUNNELS

dogs. They were still making lots of racket. As I called and yelled, they came to me a few at a time. The next day I went back to the same place, walked around and found where my young dogs had been treed. There was a big lion track leading up the hillside. We had killed a female and had a large male treed at the same time and didn't know it--one of those times when I didn't have enough faith in my young dogs

Dogs from left to right are Red, Bum, Tuffy, and Sammy,
with Cliff Hitchcock on the left and myself.

FLAG MOUNTAIN BEAR

FREDDY FERRY KILLED a big brown bear in the spring of 1978 on Flag Mountain about a half mile south of the Questa Ranger Station. Jeff Adams was helping me on the hunt, and we found this bear's track on the Flag Mountain road near the bottom of the mountain. We loped up the road and could see the dogs for most of the chase. Within 30 minutes the bear was treed. He was only about 300 yards off the road, up a steep little side canyon. I rode my horse up to the tree and could see right away that the bear didn't want to stay treed. He was in the lower limbs of a big fir tree just out of reach of the dogs. I tied my horse and got a dead tree limb and swatted the ole bear on the rump. He snorted and scrambled up the tree a little higher. I yelled for Jeff and Freddy to hurry. They had left their horses as it was pretty steep. Freddy was out of breath and couldn't climb the hill very fast. Jeff was bringing him along as fast as possible. The bear kept trying to come out of the tree and I ran him back up two or three times. Finally, Jeff got Freddy up the mountain. I told him to get on the upper side of the tree, sit down and catch his breath quickly because the bear wanted to come out of the tree. Before Freddy really had time to catch his breath, down came the bear. I hit him with a limb, but he kept on coming. I hollered for Freddy to shoot him. Bam! He shot, out fell the bear, and he tumbled straight down the steep mountain side. I didn't have time to tie any of the dogs up, so they were all over the bear. After seeing lots of bears fall out of trees, you can almost tell when he hits the ground whether he is dead or not. This bear was rolling head over heels and didn't look dead to me. I ran down the hill until we hit the bottom of a little canyon. Sure enough, the bear was trying to get up. I ran up close, stuck my pistol in his ear and deadened his nerves. Luckily, he was hit hard enough he hadn't bit a single dog that I could tell.

Freddy Ferry on the left and Jeff Adams with dogs from
left to right, Bogger Red, Tuffy, Go-Go Red.

LABOR DAY BEAR

WHILE WE WERE living at Questa, we would go down to Ruidoso and hunt with my Dad every now and then. Labor Day weekend 1978 was one of those occasions. Ted and Gary Lemaster met me at Bonito as Gary wanted to kill a bear. It rained for three days, and we could hardly get out of the house. Since it was too wet to hunt with the dogs, we decided to drive around and look at the country a little from the pickup.

Bears didn't frequent the Ruidoso dump much because it was in the low country quite a ways from the main mountains. However, we decided to check the dump anyway. As luck would have it, sure enough, there in the mud around the dump was the biggest bear track I had seen in quite a while. We waited a couple of days for the rain to stop. It kept raining, so we decided we were going to have to run this bear in the rain. We turned the dogs out on his track one morning about daylight in a light rain. The ole bear only ran about half a mile and climbed a small pine tree. Up until this time, this was the only bear we have ever known to come into the Ruidoso dump, which was just south of the new airport in 1978. People on this hunt included Bud Crenshaw, Bobby Dan and son Kenneth Crenshaw, Arvel Runnels, Ted and Gary Lemaster, and me.

Gary Lemaster's Bear, Labor Day 1978

ROBERT L. RUNNELS

Labor Day Bear on pack horse. From the left Arvel, Mr. Bear, Bud Crenshaw, Robert, and Kenneth Crenshaw.

FIRST DAY OF BEAR SEASON

IN THE LATE 1970's, the fall bear season in New Mexico began the first weekend in August. We usually spent quite a bit of time looking for bear sign prior to the first day of bear season, so we would know where to start hunting. Prior to the fall hunting season in 1978, I had been scouting around quite a bit and bear sign was plentiful. There were several places that would be good hunting the first weekend. I had been keeping track of several bears that had been feeding in the Red River dump all summer. However, I wasn't the only one who knew about these bears. For several weeks, every time I stopped to look at tracks in the dump there were always several other hunters there looking at the tracks also. Well, I decided there were going to be way too many hunters and dogs around the Red River dump the first weekend. However, I lived closer to the dump than any of the other hunters from Taos, Eagle Nest, or Cimarron. So, I decided there wasn't any use in letting these other hunters catch these bears out from under me.

The day before the season started, I called my hunters and partners and told them to meet at my house at 2:00 a.m. the following morning. Next morning, there was quite a crew; Tim Martinez, the local banker from Taos, Vi Crellin, the Forest Supervisor's wife, Merley Gonzales of Gonzales Sand and Gravel, Bob Vincent of Red River, Jeff Adams, and me.

We pulled up at the dump about 3:00 a.m. There was all kind of bear scent about, and the dogs left out up the mountain. We unloaded our horses and took off up the mountain back of the dump in the dark. There was an old road back of the dump. As we started up this road, Bob Vincent missed a turn and went crashing down the hill through the downed logs and brush. About this time, I noticed an old pickup parked in the road. Thinking it was probably hunters waiting for daylight, I turned my flashlight on and shined it in the window. Huh! Ho! There were a couple of naked bodies in there. Guess they didn't know it was the first day of bear season, and they were in pretty popular bear hunting country.

We left the old road and headed up the mountain side. I stopped to count heads, and the only one missing was Bob Vincent. However, about this time Tim Martinez realized he had left his gun in the pickup. It was now around 4:00 a.m. and gettin' close to day light. We were only about a quarter mile above the dump. We decided we better wait for daylight since it was pretty steep and brushy.

Tim and Jeff headed back to the pickup to get Tim's gun. We could hear dogs barking and horse trailers turning around down at the dump. However, there were two empty horse trailers sitting at the dump to greet the would-be hunters as they arrived. We heard about four or five rigs pull into the dump, then leave.

Three of my dogs were still down by the dump barking, Hawk, Sammy, and Tuffy. I told Jeff to check on them when he got back to the pickup. I figured they probably had a coon treed. The rest of the dogs had crossed the mountain, and we hadn't heard a sound from them for about an hour. As it started to get daylight, we headed on up the mountain. We crossed the mountain and listened for the dogs -- not a sound. We rode around till about noon and couldn't hear any dogs. Disgusted, we decided to head back to the pickup. About halfway back we heard the dogs treed in a canyon west of the dump. We had ridden past them in the dark that morning as they were across a ridge to the west of where we climbed up. Anyway, we hurried down the mountain to the tree. There were six dogs there, and they had a nice light brown bear treed. Bob Vincent was waiting at the tree for us and wanted to know what took us so long. He had gotten lost in the dark that morning and, while stumbling along after day light trying to figure out where he was, heard the dogs and went to the tree. His horse had gotten loose and run off, but he was waiting patiently at the tree for us.

Bob Vincent shot the bear, and we headed back to the pickup. When we arrived at the trucks, Jeff and Tim had another bear. They had arrived back at the truck about daylight and found my other three dogs treed near the dump. Tim Martinez retrieved his gun from the truck and killed himself a bear. Don't know how the other hunters did that day, but we ended up with two nice bear. Like the old saying goes, "The early bird gets the worm."

     ROBERT L. RUNNELS

First day of bear season, 1978. Left to right, Robert Runnels, Tim Martinez, Vi Crellin, and Bob Vincent.

BEAR IN THE BRUSH

AUGUST 1979, THERE was a big choke cherry crop in the country around Questa and North toward Costilla, and the bears were feeding on them almost exclusively. There were some large choke cherry patches in Urraca Canyon on the Urraca Wildlife Area north of Questa.

One morning bright and early, my hunting partners, who included Jeff Adams, Paul Marton, my son, Robbie, and myself, started up Urraca Canyon with my young pack of dogs. These dogs were Maggie, Booger, Bum, Tuffy, Sammy, Lea, and two new dogs bout a year old, John and Rattler.

We had only been horseback about 10 minutes when the dogs all started winding and running up the canyon with their heads in the air. All these dogs were young, none over two years old, so naturally, I started yelling and hollering, "Catch the dogs, don't let them go." Course I had no idea what they were wanting to run, and I didn't want this young crew that had been doing good lately to get on a hot deer or elk chase. I loped up the road hollering and whupin dogs back. Jeff came running up and said, "Let them go. I just saw a bear go up the hillside right over there."

We turned anxious pups loose, and that canyon echoed with hound music. Those pups set out after that ole bear like old pros, all except John and Rattler. They didn't seem to know what was going on. I only had them a couple of days and as far as I know this was probably their first hunt. There was a large cherry patch nearby and looked to be more than one bear using it. Soon the dogs split on two different tracks; part of them crossed a ridge out of hearing to the north. Bum, Tuffy, Maggie, and Booger Red stayed in the main canyon just ahead of us. During the first few minutes of this chase, my partners and I became split up for some reason or other; anyway, I was alone. John and Rattler were following me, and I was watching a mean bear chase Maggie, Booger Red, Bum, and Tuffy around on a north hillside. Finally, he came off in the bottom of the canyon, about the same spot I heard Sammy and the other dogs cross with another bear. Well, there was a big meadow there where they would have to cross. Pablo or Rob one was supposed to shoot the bear this day, but they were already too far behind, and I knew this particular bear was mean and fighting the dogs. I decided I would tie up my horse and wait for the dogs to bring the bear out in the open. I waited probably 30 minutes, and the dogs stayed in the bottom of a brushy little canyon. I decided they must be treed after all. I rode down there, tied my horse, took my gun and started toward the dogs. I remembered that my Pappy always told me, "Never go in a thick brushy place until you can see the bear in a tree." Well, I couldn't see the bear, but there were some big trees close, so I figured they had to be treed. I headed into the thick brush toward the dogs. It was so thick that I almost had to crawl. All of a sudden, here came a couple of dogs charging through the brush and both ran between my legs. The bear was close behind. Everything happened so fast, I stumbled backwards, got my spurs tangled in the brush, fell over a log, and dropped my gun. Mr. Bear had me dead to rights. However, several dogs were after the bear, and I had John and Rattler with me. John and Rattler entered the fracas, and the bear and dogs turned off to my left when they were about seven or eight feet away from me. I got up, found my gun, and crawled on through the brush until I could see Mr. Bear one more time. I put a bullet in his neck and ended another exciting bear chase.

My Dad had told me many times about a similar experience he'd been through. It happened during a November bear hunt. He was alone, and the dogs had a bear stopped on a thick brushy hillside. There were several big trees in the area where the dogs were baying, so naturally he though they were treed. Because it was such a thick spot, Pappy tied his horse and started to the dogs on foot. He was almost there, when all of sudden here came the dogs and the bear after them. The dogs nearly ran over Pappy. Surprised, Pappy stumbled and fell down trying to get out of the way. The dogs ran by, and the bear pounced on Pappy. While the bear was woolin' him around he turned over on his belly. The bear was biting him through a big heavy coat he had on. The dogs returned and were after the bear, but this didn't keep the bear from roughin' Pappy up quite a bit. Pappy had a 357 magnum in his chap pocket, and he managed to get it out and held it back over his shoulder against the bear and emptied it. This, plus the dogs chewing on the bear at the same time, got the bear off Pappy. He stood up, and the bear made another charge at him. As luck will have it, there was a large fir tree nearby. Pappy took a couple of quick steps and got the tree between himself and the bear. He moved round and round the tree while trying to dig some shells out of his pocket. My Dad was a pretty cool character; he didn't get excited very often. However, he said his hands were shaking so bad that he couldn't push a bullet into the cylinder of that pistol. Finally did, held the pistol against the fir tree and killed the bear.

This bear might have hurt my Dad bad if it hadn't been for several things. When the bear grabbed him, he rolled over on his stomach. The bear was biting him in the back and shoulder, but he had on coveralls and a heavy coat. When he emptied his pistol over his shoulder, one of the first shots broke the bears lower jaw and he couldn't bite very good.

In any case, I knew better than to walk into a thicket without being able to see the bear in a tree. However, during the excitement of the chase, one doesn't always take enough time to really size up the situation.

Maggie and Urraca bear. Maggie was about the best hunting Airedale I have ever heard of. Maggie was at the tree on more than 100 bears. A bear killed her on the Bonito near the Great Western Mine when she was eight.

ELK HUNT BEAR

IN OCTOBER 1979 we packed into the Latirs north of Red River to go elk hunting. Along on the trip was Jeff Adams, Bruce and Gary Lemaster, their Dad, and me. We packed into Bull Creek and set up our camp. It was a three-day elk hunt, and by the third evening we had several bull elk to pack out. The last evening, I was sitting on a high ridge top waiting for the elk to come out of the timber to graze. About sundown I saw a bear walk out of the timber and start up a long rockslide. He was climbing slowly turning rocks and nosing around. There are lots of marmots and pike in this area, and Mr. Bear was looking to dig some of them out of the rockslide. I walked down the back side of the ridge to shorten some of the distance between the bear and myself. He was climbing up, and I was sneaking down. I crawled over the ridge top and looked down the rockslide. Mr. Bear was now only a couple of hundred yards away. I laid my hat down on a rock and rested my gun across it, took good aim, and shot the bear in the top of the neck. He dropped like a ton of lead and started rolling down the rockslide. It was getting dark, and as long as I could see he was still rolling end over end. The rockslide was at least half a mile long, and he rolled completely out of sight. I didn't try to go to him that evening because he was too far down in a rough canyon and it was getting dark.

Next morning, we packed up our camp and elk meat. Gary, Bruce, and Mr. Lemaster packed our stuff out to Cabresto Lake. Jeff and I walked across the mountain to find the bear. We got to the bear about 10:00 a.m., skinned him near the bottom of the rockslide and took turns carrying out the hide.

A bear hide with skull and feet still intact is a pretty good load. This particular rockslide is on the west side of Cabresto Peak. From Cabresto Peak to Cabresto Lake doesn't look very far. However, it took us the better part of half a day to walk and carry that bear hide out to Cabresto Lake Road.

Cabresto Peak bear--He rolled until it got dark. Robert carrying out the hide.

ROBERT L. RUNNELS

THE BEAR'S BELLY HAIR WAS
TICKLING MY NOSE

ALONG ABOUT 1980 I was managing the Bitter Creek Guest Ranch just north of Red River, New Mexico. Bitter Creek Guest Ranch, at the time, was owned by a couple of fellows from Oklahoma. We rented horses, cabins, and guided hunts for a couple of years.

I had a good friend at Red River, Don Rhem, who had been wanting to kill a bear. I told Don several times that I would take him hunting sometime when I didn't have a hunter. One night just after dark Don showed up at Bitter Creek. He was all excited, said he just saw a big bear right in the edge of town. He said the bear was turning over trash cans where the Bitter Creek runs into Red River city limits. Naturally I asked him why he didn't shoot the bear. He said it was getting pretty late, shooting light wasn't very good, and there were too many houses around.

I told Don we would wait until morning and see if we could trail him. We decided we would meet in the mouth of Bitter Creek about 4:00 a.m. next morning. Don's wife wanted to come along, so next morning I loaded three horses and my dogs. I met them near the city limits, and they showed me where the bear had been before dark the evening before. We took a couple of dogs out of the pickup, and they could smell the bear a little. These two dogs started barking and trying to trail, so we turned out the rest of the dogs and unloaded our horses. The dogs barked around a few cabins and headed right downtown over and under porches and across backyards. It was still before daylight and house lights started coming on, and a few people came out on their porches with flashlights. The dogs headed west through town along High Street (a main street in Red River on the north side of town). We loped down High Street behind the dogs, and they finally headed northwest up the mountain out of town. When it started getting light, we were headed up Sawmill Mountain. The dogs stopped the bear on the side of Sawmill Mountain about an hour after daylight. Before we got to the tree, the ole bear jumped out and left. There was a big commotion shortly after this, sounded like the bear was fighting the dogs on the ground. This fight didn't last long, and we could tell the bear was headed east off Sawmill Mountain toward Mallet Canyon.

We headed down hill and rode up on my female Airedale, Maggie. She was lying there on the hillside sort of having convulsions. I got off my horse and rolled her over, couldn't see any injuries except for a little blood running out of her nose. My hunting partner handed her up to me, and I laid her across the front of my saddle. There didn't seem to be any broken bones so I decided the ole bear had just swatted her, and maybe she would recuperate in a little while. We continued on, and pretty soon we could tell the dogs had the bear stopped again. Soon as we started getting close and could hear the dogs real good, ole Maggie perked up and jumped off my horse. Evidently, she was feeling better, cause she took off like a shot toward the other dogs.

In a little while it sounded like the dogs were treed again, this being about the third time. I had ridden off that morning without my gun. My hunting partners hadn't been keeping up real well, and I thought I might get under the tree and help keep the bear treed. I told Don this, and he quickly pulled off his jacket and took off a shoulder holster with a 44 magnum and handed it to me. We were close to the bottom of the Mallet Canyon and Don's wife decided she would head back to the truck. I took off up the hill toward the dogs. When I got close, I left my horse and walked around the mountain side. Pretty soon I could see the bear in a big pine tree. He was a big blond bear and was standing on a big limb about 10 feet off the ground just out of reach of the dogs. He acted kind of nervous, and I could tell he wasn't going to stay in the tree very long. I slipped up under the tree and started encouraging my dogs. They were glad to see me and began to jump up on the tree and bark furiously. All of a sudden, the bear began to back out of the tree. I got the pistol out of the holster, picked up a limb and gave Mr. Bear a good whack across the rump. He gave out a woof and climbed back up on a limb. In a little while down he came again. This time I hit him with a pine knot, and he ran back up the tree. I was beginning to wonder where my bear hunter was. After all, he was the one who wanted to shoot the bear. We could both hear the dogs from where I left him.

I had probably been under the tree about 30 minutes, had run the bear back up the tree three times. Still no sign of my partner. Mr. Bear started down the tree again. I ran under the tree and hit him with a stick. This time he turned loose of the tree and dropped out right on

     ROBERT L. RUNNELS

top of me. Next thing I know, I was flat on my back and the bear was standing over me. His long blond belly hair was tickling my nose. The dogs were going crazy, and the bear was biting at the dogs instead of me. I had the pistol in my hand, so I stuck it up against what I thought had to be his chest and pulled the trigger twice. I could feel his warm blood soaking through my jacket as he crumbled on top of me. I could feel him jerking and thought he was trying to get up. The dogs were all over the bear, and I was trying to get out from under the pile. I rolled out from under the bear and dogs and got to my feet. The bear was dead. I tied the dogs back, gutted the bear, and fed the dogs. Quite a bit of time had gone by and still my hunting partner hadn't showed.

I left the dogs tied and rode back down the mountain. Don was trying to lead his horse up the hill when I found him. He said he heard me shoot and wanted to know why I had so much blood on me. I told him the story on the way up to the bear. This was one of the prettiest colored bears I've ever seen. Guess he was used to barking dogs around the houses in Red River. This was probably one reason he was hard to keep in a tree. I believe my hunting partner from Red River still has the bear hide on his wall.

Robert Runnels with a good bear near Questa, New Mexico in 1980.

BEAR ATE MY HUNTER

THIS STORY IS about a hunting partner of mine from Midland, Texas. We'll just refer to him in this story as Bryan. Every bear hunt I've ever been on was exciting. Don't even remember my first bear hunt, but I killed my first bear when I was 11 years old. Like my Pappy, I'd rather hunt than eat. Out of all the hunting we do, bear hunting has always been my favorite, probably because of the excitement. Something different happens on every bear chase. Some bears tree quicker than others, some won't tree at all. Bears nearly always fight the dogs. When a bear learns how easy it is for him to whip a bunch of dogs, he gets hard to tree. Bears leave a lot of scent and normally a bear chase is fast and furious. Dogs trailing a fresh bear track move through the country pretty pronto. One has to whip and spur to stay in hearing distance of the dogs. Length of a bear chase is hardly ever predictable. The chase can be short if you're lucky or last all day. An ole bear might run 10 miles, then stop and whip all the dogs. Contrary to what some folks might think, bears do have most of the advantage when being hunted with dogs. Anyway, we're always happy when we do get one treed.

Bryan had hunted with us many times. He had in past years killed a bear, lion, big bull elk, several buck deer, and a Boone and Crockett antelope. This particular trip he brought his girlfriend to kill a bear.

My son, Robbie, was about a freshman or sophomore in high school. He was along as an apprentice dog handler and camera man. Rob and I got the horses all saddled, dogs necked together, and we headed out behind Pappy towards Littleton canyon. There were lots of acorns and the bears were fat. Soon after we crossed into the head of Littleton Canyon, we hit a fresh bear track. The bear was headed toward Grizzly Peak. We got the dogs lined out, and soon they were gone across the ridge out of hearing. We climbed out toward Grizzly, and as we topped out, we heard the dogs treeing in a big canyon below. We got almost to them, and the bear left the tree and hauled out of there. The dogs went west around Grizzly into George Washington Canyon. When we got where we could hear them, they had treed again. Once again, we got close, and the bear jumped out and ran, headed west toward

Tanbark Canyon. Sure enough, when we got where we could hear down Tanbark, the dogs had stopped him again. We crossed down into Tanbark, and this time we got under the tree. The bear was big and black as coal. He was up in a tree that had about 30 feet of the top broke out, and he's standing right on the top of the tree where the top was missing. Looked like a big house cat on top of a telephone pole. The bear was nervous and acted like he wanted to come out and leave again. The hillside was real steep and brushy where this ole bear was treed. Rob and I tied the dogs back, and Pappy took the lady up hill to a tree where she could get a rest. After Rob and I got all the dogs tied back, I went down the hill below the tree the bear was in so I can kill him if the lady didn't make a good shot. This was before video cameras and all we had was an old Super 8 movie camera. Rob had it out so he could film the Lady Bear Hunter.

Up the hill through the brush, I could see Pappy, Bryan, and the Lady. The Lady had a rest on the trunk of a tree, and Bryan was sitting beside her also, looking through his scope at the bear.

The Lady shot, down came the bear, crash--he hit on the downside of the tree and tumbled a couple of times right into a bunch of thick brush. The bear wasn't dead and jumped up on all fours. Well, I had picked the right spot to be and when he got up, he was below me about 10 feet. I had got my pistol out and just about to squeeze the trigger and deaden his nerves, when all of sudden something ran into me from behind. Wham, almost knocked me down the hill into the bear. Well, I got my feet under me and I thought, "Dog must've have gotten loose and charged down the hill and ran into me." Then, all at once, I saw some boot heels go tumbling by. Ole Bryan, having hunted with us as many times as he had, should have known better. But, when he saw the bear get to his feet, Bryan came running down that steep hill through the thick brush, gun loaded, off safety, stumbled, ran into me, dropped his gun, and rolled up against the bear. Guess he wanted to show the Lady how brave he was. Anyway, the ole bear just gathered him up and started chewing on him. This was a big bear, and Bryan was losing the wrestling match. The bear was biting him on the chest, arms, and hands. I was standing right beside them but was afraid to shoot the bear because I had a 357 magnum, and I thought it might go through the bear and get Bryan. I was yelling at Bryan to try and push out from under the bear so I could shoot. However, Bryan was having

       ROBERT L. RUNNELS

a hard time just staying alive. I finally stuck the pistol against the side of the bear's head and shot. The bear collapsed on top of Bryan. We drug him out from under the bear. He had lots of blood on him, some of his, some of the bear's, and Bryan was white as a sheet. Rob ran up and said, "Dad, I got it all on film, but we are going to have to edit it a little because you weren't talkin' very nice to that guy."

Turned out Bryan wasn't hurt very bad. He had some teeth marks on the chest, arms, and hands. His shirt was torn off, and he had a brownish looking stain in the back part of his pants. Needless to say, his lady friend was really impressed.

We packed the bear to the house and told Bryan he probably should go into Ruidoso and get a tetanus shot. They rolled into the emergency room entrance at the Ruidoso Valley Hospital and by now Bryan had kind of regained his composure. They strolled into the emergency room and Bryan had blood all over him and almost no shirt. Course, the Emergency Room people ran up and ask, "What happened to you?" Bryan replied, "Bear got me." This was before noon, and by the time this story went through all the law enforcement radios, scanners, CB's, cell phones it got better. I finally got to town along about sundown and I heard that they're looking for a bear that mauled a man in downtown Ruidoso.

Bryan recovered and still comes to visit now and then. We call him the "Bear Wrestler" now-a-days.

MOTHER'S DAY BEAR

MOTHER'S DAY 1984 Robbie (my son), Ted Lemaster, Gary Lemaster, Glen Hagberry, and I were out looking for spring bear. We found a big ole bear track down in Blue Front Canyon which we promptly turned the dogs loose on. The dogs crossed Blue Front Ridge and headed for the South Fork of the Bonita. We decided Ted and Gary should go up Blue Front Ridge, and Rob, Glen, and I would go down Blue Front Canyon and up South Fork. This way for sure some of us would be able to hear the dogs. We figured that if the dogs didn't tree, we would meet in the head of South Fork.

Rob, Glen, and I had just started up South Fork, above the mouth of Blue Front Canyon, when we heard the dogs. We were close to the mouth of Free Gold Canyon; South Fork was running big with the spring snow melt, and we couldn't hear the dogs very well because of the noisy water. We climbed up on the ridge, east side of Free Gold Canyon, to get away from the creek. From a little high spot on the ridge we could hear the dogs barking in some cliffs on the north side of South Fork. All of a sudden, we saw a big brown bear come out on an open hill side. The dogs were all around the bear and he didn't act like he was very scared. The ole bear chased a dog down the hill. Then he ran at another dog and went into some timber. Sounded like the dogs were headed up South Fork, so we got our horses and headed for the South Fork trail.

We were excited because you hardly ever get to see the bear after the dogs and the dogs after the bear all at the same time. As we rode up the canyon, we would stop and listen every time we could get away from the creek. The ole bear was staying on the north side and still heading up canyon. About a mile above the mouth of Free Gold, my luck took a bad turn.

I was riding a green horse that needed riding, instead of my regular bear chasing horse. We came to a creek crossing where spring runoff had washed the trail out. The canyon was narrow at this spot, and there wasn't any way to go around the wash out. To cross, my horse had to jump out of the creek and climb a steep bank. We made it to the top of the bank, and my horse hung his hind foot in some roots. He fell backwards off the bank back into the creek. I was about half off when we hit some big rocks in the creek. The horse jumped back to his feet I remember thinking, "Damn, he wasn't near as heavy as I thought he was going to be." I tried to get up but my right knee was flopping at the knee joint. It was early morning, and the sun wasn't hitting in the canyon yet, and, boy, that water was sure cold.

Robbie and Glen drug me out of the creek. They found some short straight tree limbs and taped them to my leg for splints. We decided Rob would take me out to the road, and Glen would go on after the bear. They loaded me on Glen's horse and Glen took mine. I couldn't put my right foot in the stirrup, so I had to let my leg hang loose. Rob headed out, and we let my horse follow his. Took about two hours to get down to the Bonita Road. Sure was a lots of trees and bushes to bump my leg on the way out. When we got down to the road, there were several camps, so we rode up to one and asked some fellows if they would mind helping. These fellows were from Hobbs; I don't recall their names. Anyway, they were real nice and agreed to give me a ride down to brother Benny's below the lake. When we got to Bonita Lou's store it was a real busy day, and Benny was the only one there. These fellows from Hobbs were real life savers. They said they would take me on into Ruidoso to the hospital.

Back to the hunt, Rob led my horse back to Bonita Stables and reported the injuries. Glen, in the meantime had continued on up south Fork. He found the dogs treed and shot the bear. Ted and Gary heard the shot and tied in with Glen and helped him load and pack the bear out.

I had a couple of surgeries on my knee, and they eventually stapled me back together. I was in a cast for a while and then on crutches through the rest of the summer and most of the fall.

We had bear hunters, elk hunters, and deer hunters booked through the fall. I was getting around fairly well by August, but still on crutches. When the fall bear season started, I would leave my crutches at the hitchin' rail and get on my horse, hoping I wouldn't have to lead my horse through too many rough spots. Since I couldn't get around very good, I became the camera man. Sandra, Benny, and Pappy did most of the dog handling.

There was a good acorn crop in the fall of 1984, and as I recall, we caught 14 bear in August and September. We had three fellows from

El Paso (bear hunters) that could only hunt four days. They all had bear licenses, and all wanted to kill a bear. Normally, we only book one hunter on a four-day hunt. However, these fellows wanted to hunt together and only had four days. Everything went well and we took two big bears the first day and were back at the stables before noon. We rested the dogs the second day and killed a big bear the third day. Three bears in three days!

BLIND BEAR HUNTER

ALONG IN THE late 1980's, a fellow from Texas named George Evan showed up at the stables wanting to go bear hunting. Well, we got George all lined up and set a date to take him hunting in the fall. Along about September, George showed up to hunt. George was a big man, weighed about 250 pounds, and he brought a defensive tackle from Baylor along as a hunting partner. These guys were big, and we started figuring what horses we had that were strong enough to carry them. We ended up putting the defensive tackle on ole Easter and George on ole Chama, both were big strong horses.

Besides the two hunters, there were five helpers on this particular hunt. My brother Snorty, Pappy, Sandra, J.T. Crawford, and myself. We decided we're going to go over between Philadelphia Canyon and Roy LaMay's place, because there were a lot of acorns in that area. We pulled our horses down below Bonita Lake to the mouth of Philadelphia Canyon. J.T. had his jeep, so he said he'll go around on the road to Loma Grande Ranch where he could listen for the dogs if they headed that way. The rest of us crossed out behind Roy's with the dogs. We hadn't gone far when the dogs hit a big ole bear track. They headed up a big ridge towards Loma Grande with us in hot pursuit. By the time we topped out over Loma Grande, the dogs were out of hearing. When we got down to the road near the head of Maple Canyon, J.T. was sitting there in his jeep. He was all excited, said he had seen part of the dogs cross the road right there, and it sounded like they were headed right up the canyon to the west. Well, we took off up Maple Canyon and only got about half a mile and we heard the dogs treed up a steep little side canyon. We rode on to the dogs and they had a big ole brown colored bear in a tree. We took some pictures, tied the dogs back, and got George set to shoot. I got down the hill below the tree; everyone else was up hill from the bear tree with George and the dogs. Well, ole George shot and down came the bear. He hit the ground, tumbled a little ways, jumped up and headed down the hill crippled. I took off down the hill after the bear. I'd gone only a few steps when a hound ran by me. Guess when the bear fell out of the tree, ole John pulled his collar and got loose. John was right on the bear's heels, and I was running as fast as I could. John stopped the crippled bear in the bottom of the canyon, and I shot the bear behind the ear. I hollered up the hill for them to let the rest of the hounds loose. We always let the dogs chew on the bear after we're sure the bear is dead. This is exciting for the dogs to bite the bear for a little while, kind of their reward for catching the bear.

All of a sudden, Sandra came running down the hill and told me I better get back up there, that George was down. I said, "Down! What do you mean George is down?" She said that when George saw the bear get up, he ran behind ole Chama trying to get another shot, bout the same time ole John ran under Chama, and Chama kicked George.

I ran back up the hill, and when I got there George was just getting to his feet. He was walking around kind of stooped over holding his belly. He was saying, "My belly, my belly hurts bad, but what happened to my eyes. I can't see." Well, what happened was, when George ran behind Chama, he was carrying his gun about waist high, Chama kicked with both hind feet. Both feet hit George's gun knocking it into his stomach. It broke the gun stock and knocked George out. George was down and out cold. Pappy didn't know what to do to help George. He didn't have any water, so he got in his chap pocket and pulled out a pint of whiskey which he promptly poured on George's head. When George came around and got up, his belly was hurting and the whiskey in his eyes was burning, and ole George thought he was blind.

We packed George and the bear around the hill to the road. J.T. was there with the jeep waiting, and he hauled George and the bear back to the stables. George spent the night in the hospital but checked out fine and was released the next morning. He had a new stock put on his rifle and has been hunting with us several times since. His eyes are fine, and, believe it or not, he still likes good whiskey.

BIGGEST BEAR I EVER SHOT

ALONG ABOUT 1980, a fellow named Danny Elston from Oklahoma came up to Red River to hunt spring bear with me. Elston wanted a Big Bear, and I had seen a track of a very large bear in Bitter Creek Canyon a few days before. We rode out from Bitter Creek Guest Ranch one morning to check a spring where the old bear had watered several days in a row. As luck would have it, the bear had been in the spring that morning.

The dogs were fresh, the morning was still and clear. Soon that canyon was echoing with bawling hounds. The dogs headed up the northeast side of Bitter Creek. We followed along fast as we could, had to wait on Elston several times, and kept encouraging him to keep up. As we neared the head of Bitter Creek, the dogs were crossing Mid-Night Meadows just south of the Sanchez private land, headed toward Greenie Peak. Sounded like they were looking at the bear, but every time we thought we were getting close, they would leave out again. They crossed around the south side of Greenie Peak and headed for Sawmill Mountain. Several times, they stopped the bear, and he would rest and fight a while then move on. The bear made a loop on Sawmill Mountain, then turned east and crossed Mallet Canyon. By late afternoon we had made a big circle and were back in Bitter Creek almost where we had started that morning. The dogs were hot and tired, and we started catching up with them a few at a time. We had all the dogs gathered up by the time it started getting dark, except one. Ole Blue was still looking at the bear. We rode back to Bitter Creek Guest Ranch, fed our tired dogs and horses and hit the sack. Next morning, we saddled up and headed back up Bitter Creek. The dogs started trailing where the bear had crossed the evening before. About 10:00 we caught up with Ole Blue. He was old and slow but still trailing that bear. We crossed Cabresto Canyon about noon just above Jimmy Dean's upper cabin. The bear and hounds were making a little bigger loop than yesterday but again headed back toward Mallet Canyon. Just before dark we gathered the dogs up and headed for home, all except one, Ole Blue. We had passed him by about noon. Blue was around 13 years old at this time. He had been one of the best bear and lion dogs my Dad had ever owned. As tired as he seemed to be when we passed him over in Cabresto Canyon, I figured he would come on down our horse tracks to the house. By the time we got back to Bitter Creek Guest Ranch it was dark again. We had fresh horses in the corral for tomorrow, but our dogs were about done in. After we fed our horses, I fed the dogs and doctored their feet. There were only two left that looked like they could hunt the next day. I got on the phone and called a couple of my hunting pardners to see if they could come help me the next morning. I figured as sore as the dogs' feet were, the bear was bound to be getting sore footed too. Dirk Neal who lived up above Red River and Robert Reese (Zeus) who lived near Elizabeth Town, both said they would be at the ranch with fresh dogs next morning about daylight. Since the bear had made about the same circle two days in a row, I had to figure he would cross Bitter Creek that second night also. Dirk and Zeus arrived early; we saddled up and headed up Bitter Creek again. They had 7 or 8 fresh dogs. I was only able to take two that third day. About halfway up Bitter Creek, guess what I heard. Yep, Ole Blue. Ole Blue was in the bottom of Bitter Creek, and we soon found where the bear had crossed. The dogs hit the track hard and left on it fast. Now for two days I had been lagging along waiting for Elston to catch up. This day I was riding a good horse we called Red. For several years we had used Red in the White Oaks to Lincoln Pony Express Race. I still have Ole Red, as I write this story. He is 27 years old and still going strong.

Well I was tired of waiting on Elston all day, so I left him with Dirk and Zeus, and headed out after the dogs. I hung the spurs to Red and started cutting across the country. In about an hour I was ahead of the dogs and heard them coming up a big canyon toward me. I tied Red to a tree and walked down the mountain a ways. There was a big hillside with lots of blown down timber on it below me. I watched and listened a little while, and I could see the bear coming up the hill right toward me. The bear was almost blonde in color and big as a Charolais bull. I didn't have my rifle with me, and about now I was wishing I did. The ole bear would stop and run at the dogs every now and then and run them back. Then he would come on up the hill. Like I thought, he wasn't in any hurry, probably because his feet were a little sore. Anyway, he kept coming right toward me. I had a 357 magnum I kept in my chap pocket. I got it out and waited. When he got within about 15 yards of

          ROBERT L. RUNNELS

me, I held the pistol against the tree I was sitting behind and aimed for his brisket. He was coming straight up hill when I touched it off. When I shot, he rolled back over a log and jumped up. My shot was a little off center and broke a shoulder. The dogs all charged him when I shot. He grabbed a dog by the back of the neck and started shaking him like he was a rabbit. I ran down the hill, got close as I could and tried to shoot him behind the ear, being careful not to hit the dog. Bang, he dropped the dog, and his lower jaw flopped down. I hit him where his lower jaw hinged below his ear. The dog didn't seem to be hurt too bad, and the bear's jaw was broken so he couldn't bite any more dogs. Both shots, I was trying to kill him. Now all of a sudden, I decide, "What the heck. He can't get away, and he can't hurt any more dogs. Might as well go get Danny and my pardners." As it turned out, my pardners had heard me shooting and were getting close. We took Danny down to the bear, and he administered the coup-de-grace. It took all four of us to load the bear on a horse, and then the horse barely carried him down to the Bitter Creek jeep road. So far, this is the biggest bear I ever helped kill.

Robbie Runnels with Elston's big bear, Bitter Creek, 1981. So far this is the biggest bear I ever helped kill. Mr. Elston had a life size mount of this bear and the taxidermist had to use a large grizzle form.

GOT TO THINK IT WAS FUN

I N THE FALL of 1999, we were about out of bear grease. We use bear oil or grease on our saddles, chaps, and boots because it is one of the best waterproofing and leather preservatives there is. When rendered right, bear oil looks like Wesson oil. Old timers used bear oil a lot for cooking; it makes good biscuits and pie crusts. Anyway, we try to keep a couple of gallons of bear oil on hand at all times.

It was November; deer and bear season was open at the same time. Couple of our long-time hunting pardners, Jack and Beverly Walthall, were over in their cabin in the mouth of Water Canyon. Sandra and I decided to take some dogs and our horses over to Jack and Beverly's and hunt bears a few days. There weren't many acorns on the Bonito side of the mountain, and we had caught a big bear over close to Jack and Beverly's the week before.

We pulled into Jack and Beverly's early on a Saturday morning. Robbie Hooten was there and decided he would like to ride along. We got our horses saddled and headed up Water Canyon. There had been a little snow a few days before, and there was still a little left on the north slopes. We made a big circle, found a couple of lion tracks and a couple of bear tracks, but nothing fresh enough to trail. We spent the night at Jack and Bev's and told and retold old hunting stories. Sunday morning, we headed up Sanders Canyon. The dogs hit a bear track about a quarter mile from the house and headed up the canyon. The track looked to be a pretty good size bear, and the dogs were trailing like it was fresh. Sanders Canyon is rough country, and by the time we got where we could hear toward the head of the canyon, the dogs were nearly out of hearing distance. My hearing is bad, and I have a hard time telling direction. Jack, Robbie, and Sandra all thought the dogs were headed east into McIver Canyon. Not being able to tell direction of sound is a pretty big handicap. I have trailed bears out of Sanders Canyon many times, and most of the time bear head southwest into Elder canyon, However, after discussing this we decided to ride back down Sanders Canyon and listen up McIver Canyon. Because the country is so rough and brushy, it is hard to get from Sanders to McIver without riding back down to the mouth of Sanders and east around the mountain to the mouth of McIver. We did this and rode up McIver about a mile. Couldn't anyone hear a dog, so we rode back down McIver and went up Water Canyon which is the next canyon east. We couldn't hear any dogs in Water Canyon either. It was getting about mid-day by now, so we headed back to Jack and Beverly's cabin.

Jack started the generator and turned on the Sunday football game. Beverly cooked up a big lunch, and we all nested up a little. After lunch, Robbie Hooten had to head home to catch up on his chores. In the meantime, I kept wondering where we missed the dogs. About 2:00 p.m. I finally convinced Jack and Sandra we ought to ride up Sanders Ridge and listen toward Elder Canyon. Jack kind of hated to leave the football game, but jumped up, turned the generator off, and headed out. About three quarters of the way up Sanders Ridge, Sandra pulled her horse up and said, "I think I can hear dogs." Sure enough there was a faint echo. We trotted on to the top where we could hear across Elder Canyon. The dogs were treed all the way across Elder almost to Darghty Ridge.

It was getting pretty late in the evening, and we had to cross Elder Canyon to get to the dogs. Elder Canyon, like nearly all the canyons on the west side of the White Mountain Wilderness, is rough, rocky, brushy, and steep. We had to lead our horses most of the way. When we got close to the tree, we left our horses and walked to the tree. The dogs had been treed for about eight hours and were tired and thirsty. The ole bear was nervous and wanted to come out of the tree. He was running up and down the tree, popping his teeth and snortin' something fierce. We quickly tied up part of the dogs, then Sandra got a rest and shot the bear.

Well we had the bear killed, but we were in a pretty rough place and it was getting close to dark. While Sandra and I were gutting the bear and feeding the dogs, Jack headed back to get his horse so we could pack the bear out. We fed the dogs all the meat and guts they could eat; we always feed them all they can eat after we kill a bear or lion.

Jack brought ole Chief down, and we loaded the bear and Jack packed him up to the top of Darghty Ridge. It was starting to get dark, so we hung the bear in a big tree. We checked through our saddle bags, and no one had a flashlight. Jack and I each had 3 or 4 beers, and Jack had his walkie-talkie radio. It was getting dark fast, and we knew it was going to get cold. The wind was starting to blow, and there wasn't going to be any moon. Sandra and I were both riding green horses that didn't know the country, and we were a long way from the house. The good news was we did have our winter coats and gloves, and Jack had been up and down Darghty Ridge numerous times on ole Chief. We figured even in the dark, ole Chief would be able to go down the Darghty Ridge trail, and our horses could follow. However, if we could make it down Darghty to the forest boundary, it was still a long way to Jack's, and the trail from Darghty around the forest boundary is rough and brushy even in the day light. We decided it would be best to call Beverly and get her to bring a pickup and horse trailer around to the I-X Ranch, Three Rivers boundary at North Well (if we could make it off Darghty Ridge). North Well would be a lot closer than trying to go around the mountain in the dark to Jack's. Sounded like a good plan, Jack got his handy dandy, walky talky radio and called Beverly. Jack got most of the message to Beverly, and the dandy radio batteries went dead. We weren't sure Beverly got the message straight or not. Jack tried to call her several more times, but the batteries were dead.

It was pitch dark by now and we headed down Darghty Ridge, with Jack and Chief in the lead. Ole Chief followed the trail pretty good, except every now and then he would take a short cut. I've been up and down that ridge a thousand times, but never on a green horse, in the dark, that didn't know the trail. Dark as it was, I could tell every time ole Chief took a short cut, because all of a sudden there would be too many bluffs, cholla, and pricklypear. It was so bad in several places, Sandra and I had to lead our horses and kinda feel our way along. Never bumped into so many cactus and stepped off so many bluffs in my life.

We finally got close to the end of Darghty Ridge, and I knew the trail switched back several times to the south to bypass some big bluffs. I knew we were getting close to the place where the trail left the ridge top, when I stepped off a bluff and found myself hanging in the air holding on to my bridle reins. I could hear ole Chief and Jack sliding and rolling rocks; it sounded like an avalanche. I yelled to Sandra to hold up, crawled back up the bluff, and we felt our way around to the south until we found a place to slide down. In this area the south side of the ridge is fairly open, and we made it to the bottom. From the bottom of Darghty Ridge, it is only about half a mile to the mouth of Spring Canyon and Walker Well. There is also an old homestead fence that is down in places and about half up in spots. I was just reminding Jack about the old fence when he rode into it. We heard screeching, staples popping, and then all hell broke loose. Our tired hounds that had been following along in the dark, suddenly all charged toward the commotion howling and barking. Jack was hollerin', "Whoa, whoa", limbs were poppin, and the hounds were barking. It is bad enough in the day light when a horse gets tangled up in barbed wire. In the dark it can be about half spooky and really turn into a wreak. How-some-ever, thank goodness and little green apples, ole Chief didn't throw a big fit, and he and Jack got loose. Since they were now on the opposite side of the fence from Sandra and me, we told Jack to try to feel his way over to Walker Well and we would meet him there.

Sandra and I felt our way around the homestead fence and went down an arroyo until we hit the forest boundary fence. We felt our way along the forest fence until we got to the gate below Walker Well. We yelled a few times, and Jack came to us at the gate. We felt around on Chief's legs and, best we could tell, he wasn't cut up bad at all. It was windy and cold, but we were out of the brush and mostly in open country. We could almost see the road heading down to North Well. As we rode along, we wondered if Beverly had figured out our radio message. If not, we could ride on to the I-X Headquarters, which would only take a couple of more hours.

We hadn't been at North Well long, when we saw what looked like head lights coming our way. Sure enough, in a little while Mark Hendricks and Beverly drove up with the horse trailer. Beverly had brought us some snacks and a toddy, and soon Jack and I were both talkin' at once trying to tell about our excursion. Everything had turned out OK, other than a few bumps, bruises, and lots of cactus stickers.

I've thought about this trip in the dark quite a bit, and the main thing that keeps coming to mind is how smart I was to have room for several cans of beer, but no flashlight.

          ROBERT L. RUNNELS

Trent Smith packing out Darghty Ridge Bear the day after our night ride. We rendered a couple of gallons of bear oil and had some meat to go with the beans. We tanned the hide and gave it to Jack for a rug.

A LONG DAY FOR SANDRA

IN THE FALL of 1984, a good hunting friend from Atlanta, Georgia, Dick Shaffner, came up to go on a bear hunt. Riding along on the hunt were my Dad, Sandra, Pug Eckland, Snorty, Mike Romero, and myself. I was still pretty crippled up from a horse wreck back in the spring. Some of the dogs we had on the hunt were Rock, Gila, Jigger, John, Joe, Homer, and Zeb. We headed up Turkey canyon bright and early one morning and we turned the dogs loose on a big bear track close to the head of Turkey Canyon. The dogs and the bear soon crossed into Water Canyon. When we topped out, we could hear the dogs crossing out of Water Canyon into McIver Canyon. Sandra, Dick, and I decided we would ride down Water Canyon. This way we could ride up McIver Canyon from the bottom if we needed to. Pappy, Pug, Snorty, and Mike stayed up on top so they could listen down McIver, Water, and Sanders Canyons.

Sandra, Dick, and I rode down Water Canyon trail. About halfway down we could hear ole John; he was getting pretty old and was way behind the rest of the dogs and the bear. We heard John cross several canyons including McIver, so we continued around to Walthall's cabin in the mouth of Sanders Canyon. Here we rested a while and watered our horses and couldn't hear any dogs up Sanders. Decided we ought to climb up Sanders Ridge and listen south toward Elder Canyon. About halfway up Sanders Ridge, we could see the Crest Trail above the rim in the head of Sanders. Several people on horseback were riding north back toward Water Canyon. I got my field glasses out and, sure enough, it was Pappy, Snorty, Pug, and Mike. It was about 2:00 in the afternoon, and I figured they must have heard the dogs loop back toward Water Canyon. It was too late for us to head back to Water Canyon as our horses were about wrung out. We climbed on up Elder Ridge, when we topped out, it was about 4:00 p.m. Our horses were tired and so were we, so we stopped on the rim to rest a while. There were fresh horse tracks around under the trees and it looked like Pappy and crew must have been in this same spot most of the day. Right away we heard the dogs down under some bluffs in the head of Sanders Canyon. Where the dogs sounded to be was real brushy and steep. The brush in this area consists of oak, locust, gooseberry, buck brush, and stinging nettle about six feet high and lots of prickly pear and dagger yucca. Not a fun place to stroll around in. The dogs sounded like they were treed. We got back on our horses and dropped back down Elder Ridge to a big saddle directly above the dogs. We couldn't figure why Pappy and Snorty had left; they had to have been listening to the dogs all morning.

Anyway, the country was too rough to try to lead our horses to the dogs, I was still too crippled up to walk down to them myself, so Sandra got her gun and told Dick to get his and come on. Before they left, I told them to be careful, that the bear might not be treed, he could just be bayed up in that thick brush fighting the dogs. I also told them if I heard them shoot, I'll lead the horses back to Walthall's and come up Sanders Canyon and try to tie in with them somewhere in the canyon bottom.

I had been sitting there with the horses about 30 minutes when I heard two quick shots. Normally this means there is a dead bear on the ground. At any rate, decided I probably ought to lead the horses down. In rough country, it's hard to lead one horse and fight the brush, too. I tied Dick's horse to Sandra's horse's tail and headed down Elder Ridge. When I got to the bottom of Sanders Canyon, just above Walthalls, I headed up the canyon. I led both horses as far as I could. Finally, I tied the hunter's horse to a tree and led Sandra's horse on up the canyon. In the head of Sanders Canyon, there is a little seep. Sandra and Dick were waiting near the spring with a big brown colored bear. Dogs were lying all around in the shade, some so chewed up they couldn't even get up.

The bear was too big for the three of us to load, so we decided to skin him on the ground and carry the hide out. Since I was still limping around pretty bad and my crutches were at the stables, I had to scoot around on my butt to skin the bear. While I was skinning, Sandra told me the story of the kill.

When she and Dick got down in that thick brush on the hill side, the first thing she noticed was all the grass and stinging nettle was tromped down in an area 'bout half an acre in size. This was because the bear had bayed up there for quite a while fighting the dogs. The bear had finally got tired fighting and climbed an oak tree, about ten inches in diameter. He was in this small oak when Sandra and Dick arrived. The bear wasn't very high, just high enough to be out of the dogs' reach. Sandra could tell they had been fighting for quite

                    ROBERT L. RUNNELS

a while. The bear was in too small of a tree, and he didn't look like he was going to stay there much longer. She told Dick to get where he could see the bear and shoot him. Dick threw his gun up to his shoulder, aimed, and let his gun back down and said, "All I can see is hair." Of course he had a 9-power scope, and they were pretty close. Sandra handed him her 30-30 and told him to make a good shot so the bear wouldn't kill any dogs. Dick shot and quickly shot again. The bear fell out of the tree. The bear hit the ground, and the dogs piled on him biting and pulling hair. Thank goodness, the bear was dead when he hit the ground.

The bear weighed close to 500 pounds. It was getting late, and they were about half a mile from the canyon bottom. Sandra leaned her gun against a tree and started rolling, tumbling, and dragging the bear and dogs down the hill. She would work the bear and dogs down the hill through the sticker bushes and stinging nettle for about 200 yards at a time, then walk back up the hill and get her gun and start dragging and tumbling the bear again. Dick was tired and overweight and not too much help. When she finally got the bear and dogs down to Sanders Spring, she was one wrung out Lady.

It was almost dark when we got the bear skinned. Sandra and I rode, and Dick had to walk down the canyon to his horse. We were trying to hurry so we could get out of that rough canyon before dark. About halfway down Sanders Canyon, it was getting almost too dark to see. The dogs were limping along, sore footed, tired, three or four with bear bites that needed doctoring. All of a sudden, they hit another bear track. They all perked up like they hadn't even been hunting; bawling and barking, they head west over the ridge. I yelled and hollered but couldn't call any of them back. There was only one dog that didn't trail out of Sanders Canyon, ole Gila. He was so chewed up from fighting that day he couldn't even untrack when we left the bear carcass.

The dogs were over the ridge and out of hearing. Nothing we could do but head on for Walthall's Cabin. It was an hour or so after dark when we rode into Walthall's. We kept a key to the cabin just in case we might need to spend the night. Looked like this was going to be one of those occasions. However, we knew Pappy and everyone at home would be worried about where we were. We decided that Sandra and Dick could feed and put their horses in the corral, then go to the house and round up something to eat. I would ride on down in the dark to the Finley Cow Camp and try to call out on the phone. The Finley Cow Camp is on the I-X Ranch. The Stephenson family, owners of the I-X, have been friends of ours for years. We had stayed at the Finley and hunted deer in the fall a good many years. At any rate, I knew there was a phone in the Finley barn. It's only about a mile and a half from Walthall's down to the Finley. I was tired, my leg was hurtin', and it seemed like ten miles. When I got to the Finley, I drug myself in and found the phone. I first tried to call the I-X Ranch to let them know what was going on. No answer. I then tried to call Snorty, no answer. I knew I couldn't call Pappy because there isn't any phone line at Bonita Stables. Decided I would try Jack Hefker in Carrizozo. Jack answered, the phone and I explained our situation. He said he had just seen Snorty at a girls' basketball game there in Carrizozo. He said he would run back and try to catch him before he left town. I told him to tell Snorty to pull a horse trailer around to Walthall's and pick us up the next day.

I felt better about getting the message out so someone would know where we were. 'Bout then, I remembered an ole bottle of rot gut whiskey that some deer hunters had left. It was real poor rot gut, and nobody would drink it. I found a lantern, lit it, and crawled up in a chair. Sure as frog whiskers, it was still there on the top shelf of the cabinet above the sink. I got it down and took a big swig. Dang, it was bad stuff. I had several more swigs before I got to the first gate above the Finley. Already my leg felt better, didn't even hurt when I got off to open the gate. Halfway back to Walthall's, I had drunk about half of the bottle. Everything seemed rosy. I was singing to myself and howlin' at the moon.

Next morning, all the dogs had come in and were lying around lickin' their feet, all except ole Gila. We fed them and doctored bear bites on several. Then Sandra and I rode back up Sanders to check on Gila. He was still close to the bear carcass. I had to carry him out on my horse.

Snorty was waiting at Walthall's when we got back. We loaded horses, dogs, and the bear hide and headed for Bonito Canyon. On the way home Snorty told us "The rest of the story."

Pappy, Pug, Snorty, and Mike had listened to the dogs fightin' the bear for several hours. They decided the bear wasn't ever going to tree. The dogs had been baying in the same brushy thicket for quite a while.

　　　　ROBERT L. RUNNELS

They were up on a high rim where they could see lots of country and kept thinking they would see the bear fighting the dogs sooner or later. Finally, they convinced Mike to take his gun and walk down there to see if he could get a shot at the bear. Mike headed down through the brush toward the dogs. About an hour later, Mike crawled back up over the rim, huffin', puffin', and sweatin'. He got close enough to hear the bear growlin' and snortin' and could see the tops of the bushes shaking back and forth where the bear and dogs were fighting. Mike decided he was close enough and scrambled back up the hill. He reported to the rest of the crew that the bear sounded like he was in a pretty bad humor. They sat around a while longer and decided the dogs would finally get tired of that ole mean bear. The dogs had about quit barking anyway, so they headed home.

This ole bear had probably seen hound dogs before and wasn't wanting to climb a tree. In a case like this, the dogs will normally get hot, tired, and quit barking. When dogs get close to an old, dog-wise bear, he might run a while until he finds a good defensive position. Often, he will stop and fight in a thick brushy spot where the dogs can't see him until it's too late. This particular bear evidently had been charging out of the thick cover and ambushing dogs almost all day.

Back at the stables, Pappy was glad we had killed the bear. He was a little surprised that Sandra had gotten Dick close enough to shoot. We packed the bear skin and sent Dick back to Atlanta with a fine trophy.

Sandra grew up in the southwest part of Kansas, near the little town of Elk Heart. For a girl from the flat lands of Kansas, she has become quite a hunter. Sandra came to New Mexico when she was just out of high school. She went to work for me, wrangling dudes at the Bitter Creek Guest Ranch near Red River. She was good with horses and took to hunting and the mountains like a duck to water. Sandra is a better tracker than most men. If we get separated on a bear or lion hunt, Sandra can bring the hunter and trail my horse like a hunting dog. She can also trail a crippled deer or elk as good as any Indian scout who ever lived.

Robert and Sandra with Dick Shaffner's bear in front
of Jack and Beverly Walthall's cabin, 1984.

ROBERT L. RUNNELS

BEAR BROKE SANDRA'S ARM

I N NOVEMBER 1991 we had a hunter from Texas named Jack Burger who wanted to bag a bear with his bow. We have, through the years, taken lots of bow hunters for bears, lions, and elk. We like bow hunters and enjoy hunting with them. Several years back, a good hunting friend of mine, Frank Scott from Alvin, Texas, took a bull elk while hunting with me that scores in the top ten in Pope and Young Record Book. A noted author and avid bow hunter named Ray Bronk did a five-page article that was published in Bow Hunter World (September 1991) about a bull elk Sandra called in for him. Bow hunters have to be up close to their intended game, and most like shots of 20 to 40 yards. Nothing can get your adrenalin up more than being in next to a screaming, bristled-up bull elk at 15 to 20 yards, or a big bear or lion at 30 feet. Sometimes we get a little frustrated when a hunter gets so excited that he can't even draw his bow. However, if one doesn't get excited now and then, what's the use of going hunting? Normally bow hunters are good shots and, at the right distance, are pretty deadly with an arrow.

Jack Burger arrived at our house in Capitan the night before his hunt, and we planned to ride out horse back the next morning from Bonito Stables. It snowed a little during the night; there were about three inches of new snow on the road just at daylight as we drove around Bonito Lake headed for the stables. About a mile below the sables just above the mouth of George Washington Canyon, there was a big bear track in the road. Looked like the bear had just crossed the road; his track in the snow was fresh. We got out, looked at the track which was headed south across Bonito Creek. We hurried on up to the stables, loaded some dogs, rushed back, and put them on the track. The track was fresh enough, and the dogs left on it like a house afire. Sandra said she would stay and listen to the dogs while Jack and I went back to the stables to get our horses. Didn't take us long to saddle up and lope back down the canyon where Sandra was waiting. Sandra said she could still hear the dogs and thought maybe they were treed. We listened a while and, sure enough, sounded like they were treed close to the top of a big ridge between Bonito Creek and Dark Betsy Canyon. The country is extremely steep in this area with a lot of thick brush and timber. We mounted our horses and headed toward the dogs. Bout half a mile up the mountain, it got too steep and brushy for our horses, so we tied them and headed on up the mountain on foot. Jack wasn't used to our climate and elevation and couldn't climb very far without stopping to rest. Sandra stayed with Jack, and I climbed on to the dogs. The bear was a big boar; he was in a big fir tree sitting on a limb about 20 feet from the ground. The dogs could see him good and were making lots of noise. Sandra brought Jack along as best she could. The snow was just enough to make that steep, brushy hillside pretty slick. When she got Jack up to the tree, we told him to catch his breath while we tied the dogs back. The bear looked tremendous big. Jack was excited, tired, and out of breath. He had slipped and fallen so many times climbing the hill that he only had four arrows left that weren't bent. After tying the dogs back as best we could, Jack had surveyed his arrows and caught his breath a little. We told him to shoot the bear straight through the center of the brisket. Jack drew back on his bow, kinda wobbly like, and whop! Shot the bear through the belly!

I had my 30-06 and Sandra had brought her 30-30. While we were tying the dogs back, I had leaned my gun up against a tree downhill from the bear tree. When Jack was gettin' ready to shoot, I had borrowed Sandra's 30-30 so I could kill the bear if he came out of the tree crippled. When Jack shot, the bear wolfed and snorted a couple of times and climbed up the tree about 80 feet or so. The limbs were thick, and we couldn't see the bear from beneath the tree. We told Jack to climb the hill above the bear and maybe he could shoot from the hillside to the tree. Sandra moved back out of the way, and I stayed under the tree in case the bear decided to come out. The bear had gone so far up the tree that Sandra and I couldn't see him. Jack was up hill and we couldn't see him either. In a little while a piece of arrow shaft about a foot long with fleching, came falling down through the limbs; we still couldn't see the bear. All of a sudden Jack hollered down, "Shoot him, I'm out of arrows."

The bear was still up the tree. I would have shot him if he had tried to come out crippled. I figured, "Heck, he's Jack's bear. He's supposed to be the hunter." So I decided to send him the gun. If he couldn't kill him with his bow, I didn't think he could kill him with Sandra's 30-30 either because it had open sights. I asked Sandra to go down the hill and get my 30-06 and take it to Jack. Maybe he could hit the bear with it because it has a scope. Sandra walked downhill a ways and got my gun and started back up. I guess one of Jack's arrows had punctured the bear worse than his first shot had because just as Sandra crossed under the bear tree, the bear started fallin' out of the tree. Sandra heard the limbs breaking and started scrambling around the hill trying to get out of the way. It was a steep hillside and slick with snow. Sandra was out away from the tree about 30 feet when she lost her footing and slipped down. The bear was falling out of the tree from about 80 feet; about halfway down the bear hit a big limb. The limb broke and bounced the bear off to the side. The bear weighed right at 500 pounds, and he hit the ground right next to Sandra. When the bear hit the ground, one of his front legs flopped and hit Sandra across the arm. Thank goodness, the bear didn't hit her solid or it would have killed her for sure. The bear and Sandra were both stunned for a few seconds. Then the bear got to his feet, and he was standing right over Sandra. He didn't have time to bite her because I shot him through the neck. Sandra sat up holding her arm, and it was obvious that her arm was broken, as it was hanging down at a right angle just above her wrist. Jack and I rolled the bear out of the way, and I found a short tree limb for a splint. I had some black tape in my pocket and splinted her arm best I could, then took my neck scarf and made her a sling. She was hurting pretty bad, so I told Jack to start rolling the bear off the mountain and headed down hill with Sandra. She had to walk about half a mile down that slick, steep mountain to get to our horses. Once we got to the horses, I helped her on her horse and led him so she would have one hand to fight the brush and limbs.

We made it to the house fine, told Pappy what had happened and headed to the hospital in Ruidoso. We drove up to the emergency room entrance. A little nurse met us at the door, Sandra looked pretty pale and had her arm in a sling. The nurse came running up and asked, "What happened to you honey?" I looked at her and answered, "You wouldn't believe it if I told you." The nurse quickly responded, "What happened? I've heard everything there is." I looked at her once more and said, "Bear fell on her." All the little nurse could say was, "Ah sh--," as she turned and walked away.

The doctor worked on Sandra for several hours, trying to set the bones back halfway straight. He finally casted it and told Sandra he might have to do some surgery if it didn't heal right. The arm healed, but it still hurts Sandra at times. It was broken in five places.

Pappy and Curly Dixon helped Jack get the bear to the stables. Next day Jack headed back to Texas with his trophy.

Jack Burger's big bear that broke Sandra's arm.

                    ROBERT L. RUNNELS

LUCK IS PART OF THE FUN

IT DOESN'T MATTER what you're hunting, luck usually plays a big part in what happens. I've never been real lucky when it comes to being in the right spot at the right time. Normally when we are hunting lions in the wintertime, I figure out where I should have been yesterday or the day before that. I like to ride with people who I know are lucky.

Several of my friends and hunting pardners have always brought me luck when we hunt together. Shirley Goodloe, Lady Rancher and good friend of mine, has gone lion hunting with me several times. Each time Shirley rode with me we caught a lion the first day.

Kevin Larabee a rancher from Meade, Kansas has gone lion hunting with me on three different occasions, and we caught a lion the first day all three times. Besides being good people to ride the hills with, they must keep a lucky rabbit's foot. Wish they could ride with me more often. Another of my good pardners and hunting friends is Fred Payton from Capitan, New Mexico. Fred loves to hunt and fish about as much as anyone I can think of. He is also one of the luckiest men I know. Fred can almost always draw about any hunt he applies for. He is a good hunter and has a lot of natural ability. When you add a little luck to his ability, it makes for a great hunter. Fred guides a few hunters for me and always does exceptionally well. Fred can ride out in a blinding blizzard with only 30 yards of visibility, and he'll ride up on a bull elk lying under a tree. Besides being a good hunter, Fred is a good guy, friendly, polite, witty, and fun to be around. Hunters who hunt with Fred are normally successful, have a good time, and want to come back. Hope Fred can figure out how to help me for a lot more years to come.

START UM WHEN THEY ARE YOUNG

MY SON, ROBBIE, started hunting pretty young, like most men in my family. Rob passed the hunter safety course, written test, and shooting part when he was seven years old. However, he didn't get a hunter's safety card until he was eight.

We were living at Questa Ranger Station when he officially graduated hunter safety. The first year he had a deer hunting license, at age eight. We went up to Urraca Wildlife Area north of Questa to go hunting. We rode southeast from the Urraca headquarters before daylight. When it started to get light enough to see, we were quite a ways up the mountain. There was snow on the ground, and we started to notice a few deer tracks. I rode out on a bluff where we could see across a couple of canyons. We tied our horses, got our guns, and walked down hill to a spot on the bluff where we could see a lot of country. It was kind of cold sittin' on that bluff in the snow. We hadn't been there long when we spotted some deer grazing around the hill below us. I could see several does and one forked horn buck. I got Rob down over a big rock with his 243 Remington where he could get a rest and asked if he could see the buck. "Yea Dad, I can see him," he said. I told him to put the cross hairs right behind his shoulder and squeeze the trigger. The buck had stopped broadside. Bang. Rob pulled the trigger. The buck jumped straight up in the air and took off around the hillside. He only ran about 50 yards and rolled off the hill. Rob was almost beside himself and wanted to run down there right away. I told him there wasn't any hurry. We could sit there and watch him a little while. I got Rob calmed down a little, and we talked about picking out some landmarks near the buck so we could find him easy. When we got down to the buck, we took some pictures of a happy hunter with his first deer. We loaded the buck on Rob's horse and packed him out to the pickup.

It wasn't a very big buck, but Rob was as proud as if it was the world's largest. He made a good shot, and we knew this was a good confidence builder. During the following year, Rob and I hunted coyotes and rabbits and practiced shooting. Rob couldn't wait for his second deer season to start.

November finally rolled around. Rob and I discussed several times, places where we might go look for a couple of bucks. However, Rob didn't think we ought to go anywhere except back to Urraca. He was convinced that was the best place in the world.

Just before the season, my brother-in-law Paul Martin from Tulsa called and said he and a friend would like to come go hunting. I told them to come on, that we had plenty of horses. First morning of deer season was similar to the year before, cold, windy with snow on the ground. The four of us left Urraca before daylight and rode back toward the spot Rob had killed his buck the year before. Soon as it got daylight, I asked Rob if he remembered how to get to his shooting bluff. "Yeah, Dad, it's just right around the hill and down that ridge." I told him to take Pablo and his friend and go get on the bluff. I would give them 'bout 30 minutes. Then, I would ride through the timber up canyon from the bluff and maybe run some deer out.

I gave them time to get situated and started around the hill. I had barely hit the timber when I heard "Bang, Bang" a little pause and then, "Bang," a third shot. I rode out in a little open place where I could see the shooting bluff. Rob was headed down the hill with his gun. He looked like he was in a hurry, and I headed around the hillside to meet him. Snow was about a foot deep, so when I found his tracks, it wasn't hard to trail him. I rode down Rob's tracks and soon found him admiring a big 10-point buck. Rob was so excited he started telling me what happened so fast I had to get him to repeat two or three times before I could comprehend. He had ridden down close to the shooting bluff, tied his horse, got his gun and walked down to the bluff. Pablo and pardner hadn't even got off their horses. They probably didn't think a nine year old kid knew what he was doing. Anyway, Rob had barely got down on the bluff when a big buck came bouncing down the hill. I could tell by the tracks in the snow there were two deer that came down the hill. Rob said, "Dad you should have seen the first buck. He was a monster. I missed him two shots." When the second buck came out, he had killed him his first shot. The buck was a big 10 point, but Rob couldn't quit talking about the one he missed. I told him he ought to be plum proud of the one he killed. All he could say was, "Ah, Dad, you should have seen the first buck." I walked down his track a ways to make sure that he wasn't hit, and it was a heck of a big track. When I got back to Rob, I asked why Pablo didn't shoot. Rob told me that they

    ROBERT L. RUNNELS

had stayed up the hill sitting on their horses. "But, Dad, you should have seen them come running down that hill when I started shooting." Needless to say, I ribbed Pablo and Pardner for quite a while about letting a nine-year-old boy outdo them.

The next year when Rob was ten, I took him on a bear hunt and he killed a black bear that weighed close to 400 pounds. Rob and his bear made the Taos News, with picture and hunting story on the front page. Most people couldn't believe that a ten year old boy really killed a bear. Actually, he was a pretty seasoned hunter at ten and could shoot plenty good.

The following year when Rob was 11 years old, we moved to Red River to run the Bitter Creek Guest Ranch. Along in the spring, I had a bear hunter who came to hunt spring bear with me for a few days. First day out we treed a sow and two cubs, took some pictures, and pulled the dogs off. The second day out we failed to find a track we could trail. The hunter only had four days to hunt so on the third day we pulled out of Bitter Creek way before daylight. We headed down south of Questa to look around Flag Mountain. This was on a Saturday, and Rob was home at Bitter Creek Guest Ranch. We kept a old open top 4-horse trailer across the creek from the houses. This trailer was kind of our garbage trailer, and at the time was about half full of garbage sacks. Along about 9:00 a.m. that Saturday morning, Rob was outside getting ready to go for a ride on his 3-wheeler. He happened to look across the creek, and there was a big black bear trying to get in the garbage trailer. He promptly jumped off his 3-wheeler, ran in the house, and got his gun. Bear season was open, and he had his bear license. Dad had been too busy to take him bear hunting, so he decided no use to let his tag go unused. He stalked across the parking lot, got a rest on the hitching rail and shot the bear. The ole bear fell over and started kickin' first shot. Feeling pretty much the big hunter, Rob ran down to the dog pens and got several young hounds that his Dad had left at home. He took them over to the bear and let them sniff his trophy for a little while. Rob's Mom had heard the shot; when she investigated and found Rob had killed a bear almost in the yard, she got more excited than Rob. They took some pictures, gutted the bear, loaded him on the 3-wheeler, and hauled him to the barn.

The bear hunter and I had let the dogs get away that morning on a fresh bear track backwards. We rode for three or four hours before we finally saw the track and decided we were going the wrong way. It took another hour or two to round up the dogs. By the time we rode back where we had started the track, it was too late to try to trail the right direction. We rode on back to the pickup and trailer, loaded our tired horses and dogs and headed home.

The home crew had been hoping all day that we would get another bear because they did not know how to break the good news if we didn't. Sure enough, the tired hunters arrived home empty handed. It had been hard enough to explain to the hunter why we went so far backwards before I figured out what was wrong. Then we talked all the way home about where to go tomorrow, and low and behold, when we drove up to the house my 11-year-old son had killed a bear in the front yard. Try to explain how that happened to a tired hunter.

Today Rob is one of the best guides I have, still a good shot, and avid hunter. I think it helps to, "Start-um-young."

Robert and Robbie at age three, Beaverhead bear.

     ROBERT L. RUNNELS

Robbie and Maggie with Robbie's first
bear near Questa, New Mexico.

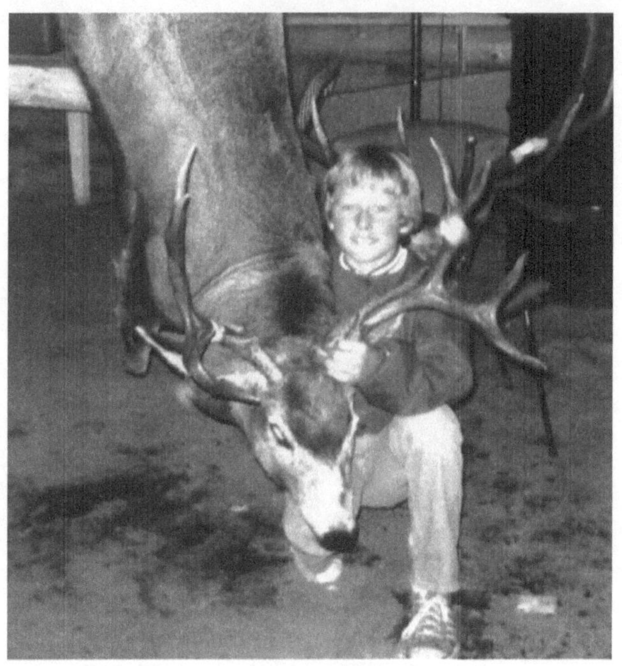

Robbie and his second buck at age 9.

ROBERT L. RUNNELS

Robbie and the bear he killed in the front yard at age 11.

THE DAY I TRADED FOR BOOGER RED

M R. NORM MUELLER, a contractor from Albuquerque, contacted me and said he wanted his son to kill a bear. We got a hunt lined up, and after I got some bear sign located, I called Mr. Mueller. I also called my long time pardners from Amarillo.

Ted and Bruce Lemaster drove up to my house the morning of Bucky Mueller's hunt. Ted and Bruce brought along a little Redbone Hound they wanted me to try out. This little red hound's name was Booger Red. Ted told me they had talked an old coon hunter into selling them Booger Red. During the preceding winter this ole hunter had caught well over a hundred coon with Booger Red and one other hound.

I was reluctant to take Booger Red on this hunt because I knew where a bear was watering pretty regular, and I didn't want anything to go wrong. Sometimes it only takes one dog to mess up a hunt, and one never knows about a new dog. Anyway, we took him along and started the bear out of his water hole. We were all horse back. I believe there was Jeff Adams, Ted, Bruce, Mr. Mueller, Bucky Mueller, and myself. The track was fresh, and the dogs moved across the first ridge and out of hearing in a hurry. We topped the ridge just in time to hear the dogs round the head of the canyon and come down the ridge across from us. They were really running, and Booger Red was about a quarter mile in front of my seasoned dogs. Well I couldn't believe this and said, "Damn! I knew we shouldn't have brought that red dog, because he is running a deer!" I figured this for two reasons. First, only one out of a hundred coon dogs will run the first bear track they ever smell; second, bears hardly ever run downhill toward the easy country. They nearly always head for the roughest country around, and this is generally up hill.

In the meantime, while I was hollering and cussing this little red dog, his running bawl changed to an unmistakable chop. He was barking treed! Ted looked at me, kind of smiled and said, "Reckon that deer climbed a tree?" By now several of my seasoned dogs began to arrive and take up the "treed" bark. I pulled my hat down, spurred my horse, and said, "Let's get down there and have a look!" Sure enough, the dogs had a pretty, light colored bear treed. I traded for Booger Red that very day, and he was one of my best dogs for several years.

Bucky Mueller was only 15 years old and this being his first bear, he was pretty excited. The bear was fairly comfortable in the tree, so we took our time and got lots of pictures. This gave Bucky a chance to calm down. When he got ready to shoot the bear, I took Bucky and found him a good tree to get a rest on. I told him to shoot the bear in the center of the throat as this breaks his neck and kills him instantly. Bucky's Dad asked me if I was sure he shouldn't shoot him behind the shoulder? I explained to them that I wanted him dead when he hit the ground so there wouldn't be any dogs hurt. We normally tie the dogs up, but invariably when the gun goes off one or two dogs will get loose or slip their collars. A bear hit through the heart has enough time before he dies to do lots of damage to several dogs. Anyway, I left Bucky and told him he could shoot when he was ready but to let me get under the tree first. I like to get down under the tree in case the bear isn't dead when it hits the ground. I can usually kill him before he hurts a dog or runs off. Bucky shot!! The bear came tumbling out of the tree. Several dogs jerked loose and nailed the bear when he hit the ground. I ran over to them and the first thing I saw is the bear biting my best dog through the leg. I stuck my 38 against his neck and pulled the trigger. He turned loose of the dog's leg and grabbed another dog by the head. I put my gun back against his neck and pulled the trigger twice. I mean I was holding it in the hair against his neck just behind his ear. The bear whirled around and knocked me down and ran over me. As he went by, heading down the hill, I don't know why I grabbed a hand full of hair on his butt. This didn't slow him down, and he merrily jerked me farther down the hill on my belly. Off the hill and through the brush went the dogs and bear. We had no choice but to turn the rest of the dogs loose. As luck would have it, suffering from a broken shoulder, the bear climbed another tree. We got Bucky down to the tree, and he killed the bear on the second try. All three of my shots had missed the neck bone. Neither of my dogs were hurt very bad. The one that was bitten through the leg was crippled for several weeks but got OK.

     ROBERT L. RUNNELS

Bucky Mueller's bear.

Robert Lloyd Runnels

I WAS BORN DECEMBER 14, 1943 in Carrizozo, New Mexico. My Mother was Louise Coe Runnels and my Dad is the late Arvel Runnels. I am the oldest of three children. Benny Runnels is four years younger and my sister Mary Lou is 12 years younger than I. Our homestead is on Bonito Creek just a mile below Bonito Dam.

I attended school at Capitan until my senior year. My senior year I attended and graduated from Pagosa Springs High School in Colorado. I started college at Fort Lewis in Durango, Colorado where I attended for three semesters. The next semester I attended the University of Nevada-Reno. The rest of my college career was spent at New Mexico State University where I graduated in 1969 with a B.S. in range management with a minor in wildlife management.

After graduation, I spent six months in Redding, California fighting fire with the Redding Hot Shot Crew. After Redding I took a job with the Forest Service as a Range Conservationist on the Beaverhead Ranger District in the Gila National Forest. I then moved to the Santa Fe National Forest and worked in the Supervisors Office on the Range Staff with additional duties as Forest Wildlife biologist. I moved on to the Coyote Ranger District and lived in Coyote and Lindrith, New Mexico for several years. I then transferred to the Carson National Forest and lived at the Questa Ranger Station until I resigned from the Forest Service in 1980.

We moved to Red River, New Mexico where I managed the Bitter Creek Guest Ranch for a couple of years. We moved back to Capitan and the Bonito in 1982. My one son Robbie is currently living in Hobbs where he works in the oil business. Benny lives on Bonita Creek by the old homestead, and Mary Lou lives in Maine. My Mother, Bonito Lou, lives in Alamogordo, and my Dad, Arvel, passed away in 1996 and is buried on the Runnels Ranch just off Highway 37.

My wife, Sandra, and I live in Capitan but spend most of our time on the Bonito. The only exception is when we are off hunting.

Three generations of Runnels hunters; Arvel, Mr. Bear,
Robert, Mariah, and Snorty. Hounds are Rattler and John.

Arvel Runnels

Arvel Runnels was born near Nogal Lake in 1914 and spent most
of his life in Bonito Canyon except when he was off in the Big War as
a SeaBee in the Pacific Theater. It has been said and can be verified by
many that Arvel Runnels was the best big game hunter, fisherman, and
outdoorsman in the Western Hemisphere. He understood wildlife and
mountain terrain better than any man who has ever taken a breath of
fresh mountain air.

I could write ump-teen books about Pappy, but for the time being
I will just tell a short story about one of the biggest bears he ever killed.

Several years back Sandra and I had just returned from an elk hunt
in norther New Mexico. Bear season was on, and we had missed a good
part of it. We rested a day and got our elk hunting horses scattered
around where they could rest a few days before deer season. We decided
we should take the dogs out for a little exercise one morning. Sandra and
I headed up Bonita Canyon above the stables. We didn't get a very early
start as we were still a little tired from the hunt up north. It was about
9:00 a.m., and we were just below the mouth of Little Bear Canyon.

            ROBERT L. RUNNELS

Dogs started winding with their heads in the air. We couldn't see a track, but we let a couple of dogs loose. They went down the hill and across the creek. When they started up the bank on the south side of the creek, they really got excited. We turned the rest of the dogs loose after we figured out the bear had come down to water and went back the way he had come. Those ole dogs (Blue, John, Homer, Joe, Jigger, and Rock) left out like a house-a-fire. Didn't take but a few minutes and they had crossed out of Bonita Canyon into Bear Canyon.

Sandra and I rode across the canyon and looked at the track. Sure enough, the track was big as a good size cowboy hat. We could tell it was red hot because the dogs had winded the track from about 100 yards away. We were excited and started to climb out the way the dogs went. Bad idea in that particular area because it was terrible steep and rough. Pretty soon Sandra slowed me down and told me, "Ole Red," her horse, had dinged his hoof. Her horse had snagged a sharp rock and cut a front hoof right in the hair line. It was bleeding pretty good, so we decided to head back to the stables and get her another horse.

About a quarter mile above the stables, I stopped and told Sandra to go on to the house and catch herself another horse and tell Pappy we were after a big ole bear. I cut across and headed up bear canyon to try and hear the dogs. I hadn't gone a mile when I heard the dogs raising cane, sounded like they were treed. I headed up the side of the mountain and after about a quarter mile I stopped to rest my horse and listen. Well, they were moving again. Guess ole bruin had just stopped to fight a while. Any way I came back off the hillside and headed on up Bear Canyon. Twice more it sounded like they were treed. Twice more I started to them, and they would leave again. The third time I came off the hill, Sandra and Pappy met me at the bottom. I told Pappy it sounded like the bear was baying up and fighting, then moving on. Pappy was riding ole Junior, and Sandra had a fresh horse. So we headed on up Big Bear Canyon, but we weren't ever able to get close to them. Bear and dogs crossed out of Bear Canyon, over Blue Front Ridge, and down into South Fork of the Bonito. Climbing out of Bear Canyon to Blue Front Ridge is no easy chore for man or beast. Sandra and I climbed out a different way than Pappy did. When we topped out, we could hear the dogs occasionally way across South Fork. Our horses were tired. We considered going down into South Fork, but after a while we couldn't hear the dogs anymore. It was getting pretty late in the day, so we decided with the ole bear fighting the dogs the way he had all day, they had probably quit barking. We rode down Blue Front Ridge, stopped to listen down toward South Fork numerous times. We never could hear the dogs. Convinced that the dogs had gotten tired and quit barking, we rode home. We got to Bonito Stables just before dark, fed our tired horses and went to the house. Cecilia and a couple of Pappy's old friends were there. We noticed when we put our horses up that ole Junior wasn't in his stall. Everyone at the house wanted to know where Pappy was. We told them our story about separating in Big Bear Canyon and told them we hadn't seen him since noon.

Well, I've followed Pappy around in the hills all my life, and I should have stayed with him that day. There is no good way to climb out of Bear Canyon except up the Great Western Road. This day we were too far up the canyon to back track and do that. Even though there is no easy way, I should have followed Pappy, because I know the way he climbed out was bound to have been better than the way Sandra and I took. Pappy followed hounds so long that he could almost tell exactly where the bear was going. He knew all the good crossings and how to get through the country the best and quickest way. I knew he had crossed into South Fork in time to tell where the bear and dogs had gone. I also knew when we got to the house and Pappy and none of the dogs were there, that he and those ole pups were still after bruin.

There are lots of big bluffs, steep rockslides, thick brush, and downed timber in the South Fork of the Bonito. When the dogs trail into South Fork, we always know it's going to be a long day. If they do tree, it's always terrible rough getting to them. Well, we were setting by the fire and it was a couple hours after dark. Someone asked, "Think we ought to go look for Arvel?" Knowing Pappy is riding ole Junior and how well they both know the country, I answered, "He'll be in any time now with a bear ivory 'bout a foot long." Well, sure enough it wasn't 30 minutes later, in the door came Pappy. He looked pretty tired but just walked over to the fireplace and put his foot on the hearth and started taking off his spurs. He then sat down and says something like, "Whoo-been a pretty long day." Ceil brought him a toddy, and everyone was waiting to hear his story. So, I asked, "Did you ever see the bear?" "OH Yeah, I saw him alright," and he stood up, reached in his chap pocket and pulled out an ole bear ivory, 'bout a foot long. Then he said, "Think

     ROBERT L. RUNNELS

he might be the biggest bear I've ever killed." After another toddy, he finally started to relax a little, we got the full story.

The dogs stopped ole Bruin several more times down in the South Fork. Pappy got fairly close to them two or three times before the ole bear moved on. Pappy finally had to leave Junior and set out on foot. Anyone that had ever followed my Dad through the woods can verify that when he tied his horse and headed off a-foot, the terrain was rougher than rough. Once again, the bear had bayed up in a steep canyon. Pappy was getting pretty close when ole Bruin got his breath and took off. This time, however, ole Bruin made a big mistake. He went out across a rockslide. Dogs were trotting along behind, keeping their distance and barking. Poppy got a quick shot and hit the bear in the back. The bear bellowed and started rolling down the rockslide. The dogs were tired of trailing and fighting this ole bear and had no idea anyone was anywhere close. With the gun shot and seeing ole Bruin roll down the rockslide, they perked up substantially. With renewed vigor, the dogs charged down after the bear, howling and nipping at him as he went in the timber. Pappy hurried down the hill, worried that the crippled bear might kill some of the dogs. However, the ole bear had been fighting the dogs all day, and when Pappy got to the edge of the timber, the dogs were barking at the bear but staying away from him. He shot the bear behind the ear. After gutting ole Bruin and feeding the hungry dogs, he walked to ole Junior and headed home.

Next day Pappy, Sandra, Skip Burgess, and I went back to pack the bear out. We rode as far as we could, finally had to tie our horses and walk to the bear. Pappy led ole Junior up to the bear. The four of us couldn't load him. He was too big and heavy. Pappy had a hoist in his saddle bag, so we rolled the ole bear downhill to a big fir tree. We tied a rope around his hind leg, threw it over a big limb and hoisted the bear off the ground. We then led ole Junior up next to him and finally pulled his head and front legs over the saddle. We then let the big ole critter down from the tree, tied him on, and he was loaded. Pappy started off leading Junior. The hillside was too steep, and the bear was too heavy. Ole Junior got down with the bear. We had to cut the bear loose so we could get Junior back on his feet. There weren't any more good trees close, so Skip and I started rolling the bear downhill. We rolled and tumbled the bear 'bout half a mile, finally reaching the bottom of South Fork. We again hoisted the bear up in a big tree and again loaded him on Junior. Junior made it OK this time, and we packed the big ole bear out to the South Fork Campground. We all agreed that this bear would have weighed 600 pounds before it was gutted. Pappy insisted it was the biggest bear he had ever killed, and he had killed lots of big bears.

I learned a lot from my Pappy through the years. Seems like every time we rode out together, I learned something new about the country we were in, or game, and most of the time both. His love for hunting, fishing, and the great outdoors was always his main reason for living. He always liked clear mountain mornings, good horses, hound dogs, the Dallas Cowboys, and pretty ladies (not necessarily in that order).

Arvel Runnels and Ole Blue. My Dad claimed that Blue made over $100,000 in his lifetime. This does not sound like much at today's bear and lion prices. Blue hunted and treed bears for many years at $250 to $300 a bear and $400 to $500 a lion. Blue was 16 years old when he died in 1983. Ole Blue's blood is still running strong in most of my dogs today.

     ROBERT L. RUNNELS

Arvel Runnels and Big Bear he killed in the South Fork of Bonito Creek with Ceil in the background. Arvel claimed this was one of the biggest bears he ever killed.

Benny (Snorty) Runnels

Benny Runnels, my brother, is four years younger than I. The nick name "Snorty" I hung on him way back. It seemed to kinda fit for some reason or the other, I don't remember.

Snorty like our Pappy is an avid hunter and fisherman. He is known to be a tad rambunctious now and then. But this is to be expected as he comes from a long line of halfway rambunctious relatives. Snorty is a good hunter because he enjoys the great outdoors and rough country.

Rougher the better. Once while trailing a bear, Snorty and I had been leading our horses through some rough bluffy country over in Tanner Canyon. We stopped to let our horses blow, and I commented, "Sure is a rough ole miserable place isn't it, Snorty?" He replied, "Yeah, but ain't it peaceful."

Snorty worked in the oil patch down at Jal, New Mexico for several years after he got out of high school. One day he was out at J.T. Crawford's ranch putting shoes on his horse. He had his horse tied to the corral fence with a hind foot off the ground rasping on it. A butane truck drove up, and the driver commenced to filling a butane tank just across the fence.

Pretty soon Snorty had to set the horses foot down so he could rest a little. He happened to notice a crow circling around above. He hadn't ever acknowledged the butane man. All of a sudden, he pulled his pistol out of his chap pocket, took a quick shot at the crow, and, as luck would have it, hit the crow. The crow came tumbling out of the sky and hit the ground near the corral. Benny didn't say a word, just put his pistol back in his chap pocket, picked the horse's foot back up and went back to rasping (just like this was an everyday occurrence). Snorty glanced over at the butane man, his eyes were bugged out and his mouth wide open. I guess that fellow thought he had just witnessed Daniel Boone's little brother in action. He finished filling the tank, got in his truck and drove off without ever saying a word.

While I was living up at Questa, Pappy and Snorty Ben came up to visit and hunt bears with me. Early one morning we pulled our horses down south of Questa and headed up Lama canyon. We had barely got started when the dogs hit a big ole fresh bear track. The country was steep and rough, and the bear was a dog-wise, mean ole bear.

The dogs stopped the bear several times, but the bear wouldn't tree. We were on a steep hillside with a lot of down timber, and Snorty got ahead of Pappy and me. While Pappy and I were tangled up in a patch of blow-down timber, Snorty busted out of the brush up canyon and caught up with the dogs and bear. The bear was stopped and fighting the dogs. Snorty was about 50 yards from the action.

                    ROBERT L. RUNNELS

Pappy and I were approaching the edge of the down timber, and we could hear the dogs fighting the bear up canyon a ways. All of a sudden, we heard, "bang, bang," several shots. We rode out onto a little bench where the timber kind of opened up, and there stood Snorty's horse. We rode up to the horse and sure enough, down the hill a little ways, there sat Snorty gutting a big ole black bear. Snorty did not have a gun scabbard on his horse that morning. As we dismounted to look at the bear I said, "I didn't even know you had a gun." He stood up, wiped his knife on his leg and said, "Had my pistol." He reached in his pocket and pulled out the same old pistol he had shot the crow with. As I was admiring the rusty old masterpiece, I noted the taped-on hand grips and that the front sight was missing. Trying not to sound too dumb, I asked, "Snort, how do you shoot that thing? It doesn't even have a front sight." He shoved the pistol back in his chap pocket and said, "I practice, I practice."

Benny is a natural outdoorsman like our Dad was, and he takes his hunting pretty serious. He rides and looks for elk sheds every chance he gets all year long (he has one of the best collections you'll ever see). He knows all the rough, isolated spots where the big bulls hide out. Hunters year in, year out tell me what a privilege and honor it was to hunt with Benny.

During October in the fall of 2001, a fellow from Houston, Texas named John McShan, hunted with Benny for five days. John missed three or four bulls and finally killed one the last day of the season. John had this to say. "I'm honored and amazed that I was able to have the unique experience of hunting with your brother. I truly didn't know what good horses are or what they can do. I thought I had a couple of good horses back in Texas, but I am going to sell them both when I get home."

Snorty, Robert, and Arvel at Questa, New Mexico with the bear Snorty killed with his pistol.

www.ingramcontent.com/pod-product-compliance
Lightning Source LLC
Chambersburg PA
CBHW031137250726
48655CB00002B/712